AF264611

HE FREEMAN FAMILY

GENEALOGICAL AND HISTORICAL RECORD
OF ONE HUNDRED AND SIXTY YEARS

EXTENDING FROM THE

IGHTEENTH TO THE TWENTIETH CENTURY.

BY THE

REV. MOSES D. A. STEEN, D D

Pastor of the Presbyterian Church,
Woodbridge, Cal.

Cincinnati, O
MONFORT & COMPANY,
1900

To

the memory of

my beloved mother,

MRS MARY FREEMAN STEEN,

from whom much of the information

was derived, this book is affec-

tionately inscribed by

THE AUTHOR

TABLE OF CONTENTS.

	PAGE
PREFACE .	9
MOSES FREEMAN AND FAMILY	11

BOOK ONE

MICHAEL FREEMAN AND FAMILY	12
Chapter I—Nancy Knight Freeman .	15
Chapter II—Huldah Freeman Anderson	16
Chapter III—Fannie Freeman Williams	16
Chapter IV—Isme Freeman	17
Chapter V—Isaac Freeman	33
Chapter VI—James Freeman .	40
Chapter VII—Moses Freeman	43
Chapter VIII—Mary Freeman Steen	47
Chapter IX—Charles Freeman .	61

BOOK TWO

	PAGE
JOSEPH FREEMAN AND FAMILY	68
Chapter I—Nancy Freeman Fry	69
Chapter II—Mary Freeman Wamsley	69
Chapter III—William Freeman	70
Chapter IV—Milby Freeman .	70
Chapter V—Sarah Freeman Purnell	73

MRS. MARY FREEMAN STEEN.
(Born 1810; Died 1895.)

PREFACE.

This little book was begun many years ago and whenever
suitable facts were obtained they were written down for future
use Much of the information herein given was received from
my mother, who was the youngest daughter of Michael and
Elizabeth Duncan Freeman and a granddaughter of Moses and
Nancy Knight Freeman, who came from England to America
about 1762 Many thanks are also due to Michael Freeman, of
Rarden Ohio, George M Freeman, of Blue Creek Ohio, and
Miss Minnie D Freeman, of Wamsleys Ohio, for information which was obtained by them and forwarded to me
An earnest effort has been made to secure accuracy, and make the
work as full and complete as possible, but owing to the lack of
historical data, the ideal completeness was not possible by such
time and attention as the writer cou'd give to it Whenever a
name first appears in the record it is written in full, if the full name
is known to the writer and its contracted form afterwards shows
the name by which he was called by his intimate friends   Thus
"Wilson Shannon Freeman' when written "W Shannon Freeman indicates that he was known among his most intimate
friends as Shannon" Freeman , and ' George Marion Freeeman."
when written ' George M Freeman," shows that he was called
"George Freeman In order to render it more easy for refer-
ence, the work is divided into Books and Chapters — a Book
being devoted to each of the two sons of Moses Freeman whose
genealogical record we have, and a Chapter to each one of their
children The succeeding generations are shown by Roman and
Arabic numerals which indicate the precise relationship of each
individual to the person whose name stands at the head of the
Chapter Thus, in Book One, Chapter VII, II 5 we see that
Joseph Alvah Freeman was the fifth child of James G Freeman,

who was the second child of Moses Freeman, who was the seventh child of Michael Freeman, who was the eldest son of Moses and Nancy Knight Freeman who came from England to America. This book is not intended for general circulation, but only for those of the Freeman name and relationship. These will find in it a genealogical history of the past, and one that can at any future time be easily extended, so as to include those who come after us. It is hoped that this genealogical history will prove both interesting and profitable to the families and individuals chiefly concerned, for none of us should willingly remain ignorant of our forefathers and kindred, whose lives and characters affect us more than those of any other people. The writer, after a careful perusal of the whole record, acknowledges a feeling of just pride in the good and honorable character of the family as a whole, a fact which should stimulate us and our posterity to act worthy of such a parentage and relationship. May all who read these pages be members of the true family of God, and have their names written in the "Lamb's Book of Life."

Moses D. A. Steen,

The Manse, Woodbridge, Cal., Oct. 1, 1900.

THE FREEMAN FAMILY.

Moses Freeman was born in the vicinity of London, England, about 1738. He was married in London, about 1762, to Nancy Knight, she having been born in London, England, about 1740. Soon after their marriage Moses Freeman and his wife removed from England to the British Colony of Maryland in North America, and located upon a farm near the eastern shore of the Chesapeake Bay, in Queen Anne County, not far from Queenstown where they continued to reside for many years — until death. Their coming to America was about a dozen years previous to the Revolutionary War, probably in 1762, and they endured many privations during the great struggle for American independence. Moses and Nancy Knight Freeman were both brought up in connection with the Church of England, of which they became full members, and after their removal to America they associated themselves actively with the Church of England in Maryland, near the place where they lived. In this church their children were all brought up baptized, and eventually confirmed as full members. Moses and Nancy Knight Freeman were the parents of several children, only four of whose names are known to the writer of this record as follows.

I — Michael Freeman who was born June 8, 1765, married Elizabeth Duncan January 3 1792, and removed to the Northwest Territory in 1797

II — Joseph Freeman, who was born about 1768, was married to Elizabeth Higgins about 1795, and removed to the Northwest Territory in 1797

III — Nancy Freeman who was born about 1770, and whose record we have not

IV — John Freeman, who was born about 1773, and whose record we have not

The record herein given contains only an account of the descendants of the two first named children of Moses and Nancy Knight Freeman

BOOK ONE.

THE DESCENDANTS OF MICHAEL FREEMAN

Michael Freeman was the eldest son of Moses and Nancy Knight Freeman and was born in Queen Anne County, on the eastern shore of Maryland June 8, 1765 was married, January 3 1792 to Elizabeth Duncan, removed with his family to the Northwest Territory in 1797, and brought up a family of nine children on his farm near Blue Creek, Adams County Ohio

---

Michael Freeman the eldest son of Moses and Nancy Knight Freeman was born near Queenstown Queen Anne County on the eastern shore of the Chesapeake Bay in Maryland, June 8, 1765 and brought up on his father's farm He was married in the same neighborhood in Queen Anne County, Maryland, January 3 1792, to Elizabeth Duncan, a daughter of Charles and Keziah Duncan she having been born in the same locality, November 25 1770 Charles and Keziah Duncan, the parents of Michael Freeman's wife, were also the parents of three other children as follows

I —Mary Duncan who was born about 1767, was married in Queen Anne County Maryland, to John Williams, removed to the far West in 1797, probably in the same company of emigrants nearly all the way with Michael and Joseph Freeman, and their families, and settled first in Kentucky John Williams and his family afterwards located permanently in Adams County Ohio

II —Elizabeth Duncan who was born November 25, 1770, was married to Michael Freeman, January 3 1792, removed to the great Northwest Territory in 1797, and brought up a family of nine children near Blue Creek, Adams County Ohio

III —Keziah Duncan, who was born about 1773, and—

IV —James Duncan, who was born about 1775 of whom we have no further record

Michael Freeman continued to live and cultivate a farm in Queen Anne County, Maryland, for more than five years after his marriage during which time two daughters were born. But in the summer of 1797, Michael and Joseph Freeman, in connection with a company of emigrants to the far West, undertook that which at that time was a truly heroic task, i. e., the removing with their young families from the eastern shore of Maryland to the forests of the great Northwest Territory to build homes for themselves and their children. At the time of leaving Maryland Michael Freeman was 32 years of age, and his wife was not yet 27 years old, and with two little children the oldest being less than five years and the youngest less than two years old they began the long, weary, tedious and dangerous journey to the Northwest Territory. The dangers, hardships and trials to be endured on the journey and after their arrival, may be better imagined than described. We must remember that the forest must be felled, fields prepared for cultivation, houses built without carpenters, neighbors few and far distant from each other beyond the reach of physician in case of sickness the wooded hills inhabited by every kind of wild beast and still more cruel men for the savage Indian then roamed the forest and might at any time appear with tomahawk in hand ready for bloody work. These men with their wives and little children, left the dear associations of the old home, never expecting to return, they bid farewell to those they loved, the sweet society of friends the hallowed privileges of the sanctuary where they delighted to worship and with a faith worthy of all commendation, committing themselves to the tender care and special providence of God, they set out for the far-off great Northwest Territory. At first they journeyed northward slowly along the eastern shore of the Chesapeake Bay, then onward in a northwesterly course along the valley of the Susquehanna River until they reached the eastern slope of the Allegheny Mountains which after a long weary and tedious struggle, they successfully crossed, and reached the Ohio River at Pittsburgh, Pennsylvania. Here they were detained for a while building flatboats and securing accommodations for their journey down the river. When the flatboats were completed and put in readiness, they with a large number of other emigrants to the West, went on board. It was while floating down the Ohio River that they became acquainted with a real estate agent, with whom they made an arrangement to possess their own lands and settle permanently on Blue Creek

and on Scioto Brush Creek, in what is now known as
Adams County, Ohio They landed at a place near the
mouth of Ohio Brush Creek, not far from where the
village of Rome now stands, and journeyed inland about eight
miles and located upon the east bank of Blue Creek, about a mile
above its mouth, or entrance into Scioto Brush Creek, where
they found a small but fertile tract of 'bottom' land Here, in
that early day, and in the forest wilderness, Michael Freeman
with courage and energy began the work of cutting down the
forest, preparing fields for cultivation, determined to build a home
for himself and family After several years of faithful and successful work, having accumulated sufficient means he purchased
a large farm three miles distant, through which flowed the waters
of Scioto Brush Creek — the east fork — where he permanently
settled and spent the remainder of his life This old 'Freeman
farm" is located on the main road from West Union to Portsmouth, Ohio, about ten miles east of West Union, two miles west
of Blue Creek, and about ten miles from Rome, on the Ohio
River, in Adams County, Ohio

Michael Freeman was an honest, industrious, generous
Christian man, and well respected by all who knew him After
his removal from Maryland he connected himself with the Old
School Presbyterian Church at West Union, Ohio, in which he
remained until death Although belonging to a different denomination of Christians, and at a time when religious lines were
generally very strictly drawn, he cheerfully donated the land
upon which a Baptist Church was built upon his farm, and
attended services there He died at his home on the east fork of
Scioto Brush Creek, April 14, 1835, after a married life of more
than forty-three years, and in the 70th year of his age

Elizabeth Duncan Freeman a daughter of Charles and
Keziah Duncan, and wife of Michael Freeman, as before men-
tioned, was born in Queen Anne County, Maryland, November
25, 1770, was married January 3 1792 and with her husband and
two little children one a mere babe, and the other a prattling
child she came to the Northwest Territory in 1797 — less than
ten years after the first permanent white settlement had been made
in what is now the State of Ohio She cheerfully endured the privations and hardships connected with early pioneer life in the
new country, and as a faithful Christian mother brought up a
family of nine children on the old home farm on Scioto Brush
Creek After the death of her husband, in 1835, she continued

to live at the same place with her youngest daughter Mary, and
her husband, who, in 1834, at the request of Mr Freeman had
come to live with them in their old age take care of them, have
charge of the farm and the management of all the business of the
estate   This duty he continued to perform for a period of fourteen years, or thirteen years after Mr Freeman s death   In the
fall of 1848 Aaron F and Mary Freeman Steen removed with
their family to their own farm, near Mt Leigh Adams County,
Ohio and the next season Mrs Freeman came to live with them,
with whom she continued to make her home until her death April
23 1851, in the 81st year of her age   Her body was taken to the
Blue Creek cemetery and buried by the side of her husband
Mrs Elizabeth Duncan Freeman was a woman of generous heart
and kindly spirit, an humble and devout Christian, greatly
beloved   To Michael and Elizabeth Duncan Freeman were born
nine children

CHAPTER I

Nancy Knight Freeman the eldest child a daughter of
Michael and Elizabeth Duncan Freeman was born near Queenstown, Queen Anne County, on the eastern shore of the Chesapeake Bay, in Maryland October 3 1792   When a small child
she was brought to the Northwest Territory, when it was a very
new country indeed — less than ten years after the first permanent settlement had been made in what is now the great State of
Ohio   She was never married and lived with her parents until
after her father's death, then with the family of her youngest sister,
at the old homestead on Scioto Brush Creek, until 1848 when she
removed with the family to their residence near Mt Leigh, Adams
County Ohio with whom she continued to make her home
Again, in 1865, she removed with her younger sister her husband and family to Xenia, Greene County, Ohio, and resided
with her brother-in-law Aaron F Steen, until her death in the
autumn of 1867 aged 75 years   Her body was buried in the
beautiful Woodlawn cemetery near Xenia Ohio

CHAPTER II

Huldah Freeman, the second daughter of Michael and Elizabeth Duncan Freeman was born near Queenstown, Queen Anne County, on the eastern shore of the Chesapeake Bay, in Maryland, February 7, 1795, and was brought to the Northwest Territory by her parents, when a child only two years old. She lived with her parents and spent the happy days of youth at the old home on Scioto Brush Creek, two miles west of the mouth of Blue Creek, where she grew to womanhood. Here, at the home of her parents she was married in the year 1814 to George Anderson, and died ———— To them were born seven children

I —Elizabeth Anderson, the eldest child of George and Huldah Freeman Anderson, was born about 1815

II —Dycie Anderson, the second daughter of George and Huldah Freeman Anderson, was born about 1817

III —Sarah Anderson the third daughter of George and Huldah Freeman Anderson, was born about 1820

IV —Nathaniel Anderson, the fourth child and elder son of George and Huldah Freeman Anderson, was born about 1822

V —Catherine Anderson, the fifth child and fourth daughter of George and Huldah Freeman Anderson, was born about 1824

VI —Paulina Anderson, the sixth child and fifth daughter of George and Huldah Freeman Anderson, was born about 1826

VII —George Freeman Anderson the seventh and youngest child the second son of George and Huldah Freeman Anderson was born about 1829

CHAPTER III

Fannie Freeman or Frances, the third daughter of Michael and Elizabeth Duncan Freeman was born on Blue Creek in the Northwest Territory now Adams County Ohio, March 3, 1798 She was taken by her parents when a young girl to their home

on Scioto Brush Creek, where she spent a happy youth, and grew
up to womanhood She was married at the home of her parents,
about 1817, to Isaac Williams, a son of Jesse Williams, who was
a brother of John Williams who was married to Mary Duncan
in Maryland, a sister of Fannie Freeman's mother Fannie
Freeman Williams died April 8, 1822, aged 24 years, 1 month
and 5 days To Isaac and Fannie Freeman Williams were born
three children

I —Nancy Williams, the eldest child of Isaac and Fannie Freeman Williams, was born about 1818

II —Elizabeth Williams, the second daughter of Isaac and Fannie
Freeman Williams, was born about 1820

III —Jesse Williams, the third and youngest child, and only son
of Isaac and Fannie Freeman Williams, was born about 1822

CHAPTER IV

Isme Freeman, the fourth child and eldest son of Michael
and Elizabeth Duncan Freeman, was born on Blue Creek, in the
Northwest Territory, now Adams County, Ohio, June 22, 1800,
and died at his home, in Scioto County, Ohio, April 11, 1856, in
the 56th year of his age. He was brought up on his father's
farm until he grew to manhood He was a prosperous and successful farmer, owning a good farm and having a pleasant home
on the west fork of Scioto Brush Creek, in Scioto County, Ohio
He was married on Scioto Brush Creek, October 5, 1820, to
Susannah Oppy, a daughter of David and Elizabeth Oppy, she
having been born June 23, 1805, and died at her home, August 2
1849, in the 45th year of her age Isme Freeman was married
a second time to Mrs Martha Thompson, widow of Thomas
Thompson, and whose maiden name was Martha Blair. To
Isme Freeman and his first wife were born twelve children, and to
his second wife two children, fourteen in all

I —Elizabeth Freeman, the eldest child, a daughter of Isme and
Susannah Oppy Freeman, was born in Adams County, Ohio,
October 15, 1821 and died November 13, 1822, aged 1 year
and 29 days

II —Michael Freeman, the second child and eldest son of Isaie and Susannah Oppy Freeman, was born in Scioto County, Ohio, August 1, 1823, and died in April, 1896 in the 73d year of his age   He was brought up on his father s farm, and became an industrious, intelligent, and useful man   He followed the occupation of merchant, farmer, hotel keeper and Justice of the Peace   He was married first by Isaac Smith, Esq , January 26, 1843, to Amanda Thompson, a daughter of George and Margaret Thompson, she having been born October 8, 1823, and died at Rarden, Ohio, May 29 1863, in the 40th year of her age   To this marriage were born nine children   Michael Freeman was married a second time by James G. Freeman Esq , to Mrs Sarah Jane Newland, widow of J W Newland, and a daughter of Charles and Sarah Johnson, she having been born near Dunkinsville, Adams County, Ohio, March 9, 1832   To this marriage were born two children   Residence, Rarden, Scioto County, Ohio

1 Susannah Freeman, the eldest child, a daughter of Michael and Amanda Thompson Freeman, was born in Scioto County, Ohio, December 3, 1843   She was married by Thomas Beaver, Esq   January 10 1863, to John Henry Thompson, a son of Washington and Margaret Thompson, he having been born July 2, 1841 — a farmer   Residence, near Rarden, Ohio   To them were born nine children.

I —Inez Thompson, the eldest child of John H and Susannah Freeman Thompson, was born March 3, 1866   She was married by the Rev James McNeilan, at McArthur, Vinton County, Ohio, November 30, 1884, to George F Thorp, he having been born November 13, 1860   To them were born three children

1 Roy L Thorp the eldest child of George F and Inez Thompson Thorp, was born October 23, 1885

2 Harry Thorp, the second son of George F. and Inez Thompson Thorp, was born November 4, 1887

3 Wilbur Thorp, the third son of George F and Inez Thompson Thorp, was born February 4, 1890

II —Minnie Estella Thompson, the second daughter of John H and Susannah Freeman Thompson, was born December 24, 1868

III—Laura Belle Thompson, the third daughter of John H and Susannah Freeman Thompson, was born October 5, 1871

IV—Elizabeth Margaret Thompson, the fourth daughter of John H and Susannah Freeman Thompson, was born January 29 1874, and died February 10, 1874 aged 12 days

V—Freeman Thompson, the fifth child and eldest son of John H and Susannah Freeman Thompson, was born January 8, 1875

VI—Charles Hanron Thompson, the sixth child and second son of John H and Susannah Freeman Thompson, was born October 2, 1877

VII—James Alva Thompson, the seventh child and third son of John H and Susannah Freeman Thompson, was born October 19 1880

VIII—Rosa Myrtle Thompson, the eighth child and fifth daughter of John H and Susannah Freeman Thompson, was born April 7, 1883

IX—Cora May Thompson, the ninth child and sixth daughter of John H and Susannah Freeman Thompson, was born May 14, 1885

2 Washington Freeman the second child and eldest son of Michael and Amanda Thompson Freeman, was born in Scioto County, Ohio, February 1, 1845, and died the next day

3 George Polk Freeman, the third child and second son of Michael and Amanda Thompson Freeman, was born in Scioto County, Ohio, February 11, 1846, and died September 4, 1850, aged 4 years, 6 months and 24 days

4 Mary Ann Freeman, the fourth child and second daughter of Michael and Amanda Thompson Freeman, was born in Scioto County, Ohio, December 4, 1847 and died October 11, 1850, aged 2 years, 9 months and 14 days

5 James Richard Freeman, the fifth child and third son of Michael and Amanda Thompson Freeman, was born August 6, 1850 He was married, November 6, 1873, by James G. Freeman, Esq, to Elizabeth Ann Thompson, she having been born in Scioto County, Ohio, May 22, 1850 To them were born seven children

I —Alpheus Edmond Freeman, the eldest child of James R
and Elizabeth A. Freeman, was born April 2, 1875

II —Vernon Everett Freeman, the second son of James R
and Elizabeth A Freeman, was born June 5, 1877

III —Iva Estella Freeman, the third child and only daughter
of James R and Elizabeth A Freeman, was born April 4,
1879

IV —Michael Elza Freeman, the fourth child and third son
of James R and Elizabeth A Freeman, was born April 5,
1881

V —John Crayton Freeman, the fifth child and fourth son of
of James R and Elizabeth A Freeman, was born June 30,
1883.

VI —William Buchanan Freeman, the sixth child and fifth
son of James R. and Elizabeth A. Freeman, was born
December 20, 1885

VII —Charles Leslie Freeman, the youngest child of James
R and Elizabeth A Freeman, was born October 14, 1888

6 Margaret Jane Freeman, the sixth child and third daughter
of Michael and Amanda Thompson Freeman, was born in
Scioto County, Ohio, August 1, 1852   She was married by
James G Freeman, Esq, November 25, 1870, to William
Jefferson Thompson — a farmer and blacksmith — a son of
John and Catherine Thompson, he having been born in
Brush Creek Township, Scioto County, Ohio, October 10,
1847   Residence, Rarden, Ohio   To them were born
twelve children.

I —Michael Alfred Thompson the eldest child of William J
and Margaret J. Freeman Thompson, was born in Scioto
County, Ohio, December 25, 1871, and died September 6,
1872

II —Ida Melvina Thompson, the second child and eldest
daughter of William J and Margaret J Thompson, was
born December 29, 1872   She was married by John
Davis, Esq, September 17, 1892 to James M Lanthron

III —John Davy Thompson, the third child and second son
of William J and Margaret J Thompson, was born April
18, 1874

IV —Charles Crayton Thompson, the fourth child and third
son of William J and Margaret J Thompson, was born
in Scioto County, Ohio, August 16, 1876, and died September 6, 1879

V —Cora Ann Thompson, the fifth child and second daughter of William J and Margaret J Thompson, was born
November 13, 1877.

VI —Enza Ethel Thompson, the sixth child and third daughter of William J and Margaret J Thompson, was born in
Scioto County, Ohio, August 20, 1879

VII.—Zola Jane Thompson, the seventh child and fourth
daughter of William J and Margaret J Thompson, was
born in Scioto County, Ohio, August 12, 1882

VIII —Harley Buchanan Thompson, the eighth child and
fourth son of William J. and Margaret J Thompson, was
born in Scioto County, Ohio, September 11, 1884

IX —Clara Lenora Thompson, the ninth child and fifth
daughter of William J. and Margaret J Thompson, was
born in Scioto County, Ohio, September 9, 1886, and died
February 22, 1889

X —Jesse Earl Thompson, the tenth child and fifth son of
William J and Margaret J Thompson, was born in Scioto
County, Ohio, March 28, 1888

XI —Dollie Olive Thompson, the eleventh child and sixth
daughter of William J and Margaret J Thompson, was
born in Scioto County, Ohio, October 30, 1890

XII —William Elden Thompson, the twelfth child and sixth
son of William J and Margaret J Thompson, was born
in Scioto County, Ohio, September 4, 1892

7 Isme Wilson Freeman, the seventh child and fourth son of
Michael and Amanda Thompson Freeman, was born in
Scioto County, Ohio, June 2, 1854, and died April 14, 1856

8 Buchanan Freeman, the eighth child and fifth son of Michael
and Amanda Thompson Freeman, was born in Scioto
County, Ohio, July 13, 1856   He was married by James G
Freeman, Esq, July 4, 1880, to Ida Windle, a daughter of
Grafton and Lorena Windle, she having been born June 22,
1862   Occupation, a cooper   Residence, Rarden, Ohio

9 Julia Freeman, the ninth child and fourth daughter of
Michael and Amanda Thompson Freeman, was born in Rarden Scioto County, Ohio, December 24, 1859, and died July
16 1860

10 Charles Samuel Freeman, the tenth child of Michael Freeman, the eldest by his second wife, Sarah Jane Freeman, was born in Rarden Scioto County Ohio, September
18, 1865 — occupation, a cooper   He was married by J N
Kates, Esq , at Byers Station, Ohio, November 25, 1886, to
Mary Delia Stiers, a daughter of R B and M L Stiers, she
having been born July 30, 1860   Residence, Rarden Ohio
To them were born two children

  I —Infant son of Charles S and Mary D Freeman, was born
  and died August 25, 1887

  II —Clovis Clyde Freeman, the second son of Charles S.
  and Mary D Freeman, was born December 8, 1889

11 William Alfred Freeman, the eleventh child and seventh
son of Michael Freeman, the second son by his second wife,
Sarah Jane Freeman, was born in Rarden, Scioto County,
Ohio, February 8, 1869   He was married to Dora Steward
in Rarden, Ohio, in December, 1893   Residence Rarden,
Ohio

III —David Freeman, the third child and second son of Isme
and Susannah Freeman, was born in Brush Creek Township,
Scioto County, Ohio, September 6, 1825, and died in the same
neighborhood, March 12, 1884, in the 59th year of his age
He was a successful and prosperous farmer   David Freeman
was married by George Thompson, Esq , January 27 1848, to
Martha Caroway, a daughter of Henry and Delia Caroway,
she having been born March 14 1830 and died at their home
October 22 1864, in the 35th year of her age   To this marriage were born three children   David Freeman was married
a second time by his brother, Michael Freeman, Esq , January
11, 1866, to Emily Hazelbaker, a daughter of John and Sophia
Hazelbaker she having been born March 1, 1845   To this
marriage were also born three children

  1 John Freeman, the eldest child of David and Martha Caroway Freeman, was born in Scioto County, Ohio, April 9,
  1851 and was brought up on his father's farm   He afterwards became a merchant at Rarden, Ohio, where he died,
  March 26, 1876, in the 25th year of his age   John Free-

man was married by James G Freeman, Esq, March 7, 1872, to Elizabeth Margaret Tracy, a daughter of Joseph W and Mary J Tracy, she having been born January 1, 1850 and died March 27, 1875, in the 26th year of her age. To them one child was born

I —Lovinia Freeman, daughter of John and Elizabeth M Freeman, was born in Rarden, Ohio, August 1, 1873 She was married in 1894

2 Henry Franklin Freeman, the second son of David and Martha Caroway Freeman was born in Scioto County, Ohio, December 5, 1852 He removed to the West many years ago, and has not been heard from

3 Thomas Fletcher Freeman, the third son of David and Martha Caroway Freeman, was born in Scioto County, Ohio, December 10, 1858 — occupation, a cooper He was married by J N Kates, Esq, May 17, 1888 to Julia Ann Windle, a daughter of Grafton and Lorena Windle, she having been born December 6, 1870 To them were born three children Residence, Rarden, Scioto County, Ohio

I —Ida Lenora Freeman, the eldest child of Thomas F and Julia A Freeman, was born in Scioto County, Ohio, November 15, 1888, and died October 25, 1889

II —Leslie Alfred Freeman, the second child and elder son of Thomas F and Julia A Freeman, was born in Scioto County, Ohio, September 23, 1890.

III —Cloyd Freeman, the third child and second son of Thomas F and Julia A Freeman, was born in Scioto County, Ohio, May 13, 1892

4 Sophia Ann Freeman, the fourth child and eldest daughter of David Freeman, the eldest child by his second wife Emily Hazelbaker Freeman, was born near Rarden, Scioto County, Ohio, September 20, 1867, and died October 27, 1871

5 Mary Jane Freeman, the fifth child of David Freeman, the second daughter by his second wife, Emily Hazelbaker Freeman, was born near Rarden, Ohio, February 28, 1869

6 Nora Estella Freeman, the sixth child and third daughter of David Freeman, the third child by his second wife, Emily Hazelbaker Freeman, was born near Rarden, Scioto County, Ohio, October 27, 1879

IV —William Freeman, the fourth child and third son of Isme and Susannah Freeman, was born in Scioto County, Ohio, November 15, 1827, and died in Otway, Ohio, March 25, 1895, at 2 o'clock P M , in the 68th year of his age — a farmer He was married by the Rev Mr Gatch, October 6, 1846, to Margaret Thompson, a daughter of George and Margaret Thompson, she having been born November 25, 1827   To them were born thirteen children

1   Isme Taylor Freeman, the eldest child of William and Margaret Thompson Freeman, was born in Scioto County, Oh.o, June 20, 1847.   He was married, August 18, 1865, to Lucinda Brown, by whom he had five children I Taylor Freeman was married a second time and had two children I Taylor Freeman was married a third time and had four children   He was thus the father of eleven children

2   George Thompson Freeman, the second son of William and Margaret Freeman, was born October 15, 1848, and died August 5, 1854, in the 6th year of his age

3   John Jefferson Freeman, the third son of William and Margaret Freeman, was born February 10, 1850   He was married to Martha Ann McCan, by whom he had seven children

4   Samuel Oppy Freeman, the fourth son of William and Margaret Freeman, was born May 23, 1851, and died December 12, 1853, in the third year of his age

5   Jesse Edward Freeman, the fifth son of William and Margaret Freeman, was born March 10, 1853 and died December 18, 1867, in the 15th year of his age

6   Mary Jane Freeman, the sixth child and eldest daughter of William and Margaret Freeman, was born December 17, 1854   She was married, December 20, 1877, to Jasper Wamsley, a son of William Wamsley   To them were born two children

I —Carey Wamsley

II —Clara Beatrice Wamsley.

7   Charles Freeman, the seventh child and sixth son of William and Margaret Freeman, was born August 30, 1856, and died May 9, 1891, in the 35th year of his age   He was mar-

ried July 3, 1878, to Mary Virginia James, by whom he had two children

8 Laura Belle Freeman, the eighth child and second daughter of William and Margaret Freeman, was born December 31 1858 She was married, March 13, 1879, to Hugh George Davis They had four children

9 William Finley Freeman, the ninth child and seventh son of William and Margaret Freeman, was born January 28, 1861, and died February 12, 1862

10 Margaret Ann Freeman, the tenth child and third daughter of William and Margaret Freeman, was born February 10, 1863 She was married, September 21, 1881, to John H Davis To them were born three children

11 Edward Sherman Freeman, the eleventh child and eighth son of William and Margaret Freeman, was born July 22, 1865 He was married, August 17, 1887, to Caroline Potter

12 Joseph Freeman, the twelfth child and ninth son of William and Margaret Freeman, was born December 19, 1867, and died the same day

13 Sabrina Elsie Freeman, the thirteenth child and fourth daughter of William and Margaret Freeman, was born September 6 1869, and died August 8, 1870

V —Elizabeth Ann Freeman, the fifth child and second daughter of Isaac and Susannah Freeman, was born in Scioto County, Ohio, February 7, 1830 She was married by the Rev. Jesse Wamsley, near Otway, Ohio, May 30, 1850, to Samuel Bolton Wamsley, a son of William and Elizabeth Wamsley, he having been born December 28 1829 They have resided on a farm near Wamsley, Adams County, Ohio, where Mrs Elizabeth Ann Freeman Wamsley died, October 12, 1883, in the 54th year of her age To them were born ten children

  1 William Freeman Wamsley, the eldest child of Samuel B and E Ann Wamsley, was born near Wamsley, Adams County, Ohio, August 2, 1851 He was married, September 2, 1874, to Mary Frances McCormick, a daughter of Charles and Rebecca McCormick, she having been born March 5, 1854 To them were born two children

    I —Clement Lloyd Wamsley, the elder child of W Freeman and Mary F Wamsley, was born December 18, 1876

II —Charles Samuel Wamsley, the second son of W Freeman and Mary F Wamsley, was born July 15, 1879

2 Damaris Omi Wamsley, the second child and eldest daughter of Samuel B and E Ann Wamsley, was born November
22, 1852, and died February 8, 1858, in the 6th year of her
age

3 Elizabeth Jane Wamsley, the third child and second daughter of Samuel B and E Ann Wamsley, was born March 3,
1855. She was married, September 3, 1874, to William
Legit Neary, a son of Matthew and Sarah Neary, he having
been born September 28, 1841. To them were born eight
children.   ,

I —Samuel Tilden Neary was born October 23, 1876

II —Floyd Edward Neary was born April 7, 1878

III —Melvin Owen Neary was born May 24, 1880

IV —Mary Florence Neary was born January 22, 1882

V —Essie Blanche Neary was born March 20, 1884

VI —Loy Clifton Neary was born June 7, 1886

VII —Ann Lee Neary was born October 3, 1888

VIII —Harley Pearl Neary was born November 7, 1890

4 Emma Alice Wamsley, the fourth child and third daughter
of Samuel B and E Ann Wamsley, was born near Wamsley, Adams County, Ohio, December 24, 1856 She was
married, March 3, 1876, to George Duncan McCormick, a
son of Charles and Rebecca McCormick, he having been
born October 5, 1845 To them was born one child

I —Edgar Eugene McCormick, son of George D and Emma
A McCormick, was born March 22, 1878.

5 Florence Wamsley, the fifth child and fourth daughter of
Samuel B and E Ann Wamsley, was born near Wamsley
Adams County, Ohio, December 20, 1858 She was mar-
ried to George Ryne Residence, Mineral Springs, Ohio.

6 James Franklin Wamsley, the sixth child and second son
of Samuel B. and E Ann Wamsley, was born near Wamsley, Adams County, Ohio, December 26, 1862, and died
January 12, 1863

7 George McClelland Wamsley, a twin brother of the preced-
ing, the seventh child and third son of Samuel B and E Ann

Wamsley, was born December 26, 1862, and died March 22, 1864

8 Electa Ellen Wamsley, the eighth child and fifth daughter of Samuel B and E Ann Wamsley, was born near Wamsley, Adams County, Ohio, July 12, 1864 She was married November 25, 1882, to Allen Marshall Wamsley, a son of Peter W and Sarah E Wamsley, he having been born May 11, 1860 To them was born one child

  I—Ocie Alice Wamsley, daughter of Allen M and Electa Ellen Wamsley, was born December 19, 1883

9 Dora Sabrina Wamsley, the ninth child and sixth daughter of Samuel B and E Ann Wamsley, was born near Wamsley, Adams County, Ohio, August 20, 1868 She was married by the Rev R. F. Wamsley, at White Oak, Ohio, January 20, 1891, to John A Jones — a farmer — a son of A J and Jane Jones, he having been born April 16, 1868

10 Harley Rufle Wamsley, the tenth child and fourth son of Samuel B and E Ann Wamsley, was born near the village of Wamsley, Adams County, Ohio, September 9, 1872, and died August 25, 1898, in the 26th year of his age

VI—John Purnell Freeman, the sixth child and fourth son of Isme and Susannah Freeman, was born May 2, 1832, on his father's farm, in Scioto County, Ohio, where he was brought up He was by occupation a farmer He died near Wamsley, Adams County, Ohio, April 13, 1891, in the 59th year of his age He was married by Noah Tracy, Esq, in Brush Creek Township, Scioto County, Ohio, January 9 1851 to Elizabeth Jane Jones, a daughter of Andrew B and Vienna Jones, she having been born October 10, 1832, and died April 6, 1898 To them were born ten children

1 Andrew Bird Freeman, the eldest child of J Purnell and Elizabeth J Freeman, was born in Scioto County, Ohio, June 8, 1852, and died June 14, 1852

2 Franklin Pierce Freeman, the second son of J Purnell and Elizabeth J Freeman, was born in Scioto County, Ohio, April 10, 1853, and died December 21, 1853

3 Thomas Benton Freeman, the third son of J Purnell and Elizabeth J Freeman, was born in Scioto County, Ohio, November 5, 1854 and died December 9, 1861

4 Artemisi Freeman, the fourth child and eldest daughter of
J Purnell and Elizabeth J Freeman, was born in Scioto
County, Ohio, August 8, 1857   She was married by James
G Freeman, Esq , October 27, 1879, to Isaac Dixon McFar-
land, he having been born January 24, 1847   To them was
born one child.

I—Robert Melvin McFarland was born July 3, 1881

5 Sarah Salome Freeman, the fifth child and second daughter
of J Purnell and Elizabeth J Freeman, was born in Scioto
County, Ohio, September 8 1859   She was married by the
Rev H B Hill, May 14, 1890, to Wesley Ralston, a son of
Robert and Mary Ralston, he having been born September
14, 1852   To them was born one child

I—Martha Jane Ralston was born March 17, 1891

6 Clement Laird Valandigham Freeman, the sixth child and
fourth son of J Purnell and Elizabeth J Freeman, was born
in Scioto County, Ohio, May 20, 1862   He was married by
the Rev R F Wamsley, September 27 1889, to Lenora
Liston, a daughter of George and Matilda Liston, she having been born February 15, 1872   To them were born three
children

I—Clarence Leslie Freeman, son of C L V and Lenora
   Freeman, was born July 18, 1890, and died in November,
   1892

II—Homer Freeman was born in 1892

III—Harry Thomas Freeman was born in 1894

7 Crittenden Freeman, the seventh child and fifth son of J.
Purnell and Elizabeth J Freeman, a twin brother of the pre-
ceding, Clement L V Freeman, was born in Scioto County,
Ohio, May 20, 1862

8 Donie Neosho Seymour Freeman, the eighth child and
sixth son of J Purnell and Elizabeth J Freeman, was born
in Scioto County, Ohio, April 11, 1865, and died July 31,
1869

9 Martha Jane Freeman, the ninth child and third daughter
of J Purnell and Elizabeth J. Freeman, was born in Scioto
County, Ohio, August 7, 1868

10 Cora Arbana Freeman the tenth child and fourth daughter of J Purnell and Elizabeth J Freeman, was born in

Scioto County, Ohio, August 5, 1871   She was married by
J G Hazelbaker, Esq, January 11, 1890, to John Miller, a
son of Jacob Miller, he having been born March 20, 1869
To them were born the following twin children.

I —Charles Crittenden Miller, son of John and Cora A
Miller, was born March 25, 1891

II —Obada Bethel Miller was born March 25, 1891.

VII —James Fletcher Freeman, the seventh child and fifth son
of Isme and Susannah Freeman, was born at Otway, Scioto
County, Ohio, September 13, 1834 — by occupation a black-
smith   He was married by the Rev. Mr Tole, near West
Union, Adams County, Ohio, December 20, 1857, to Sabrina
Elizabeth Hazelbaker, a daughter of Joseph and Sarah A
Hazelbaker, she having been born in Rome, Adams County,
Ohio, June 6, 1841   To them were born four children

1. Minnie Delle Freeman, the eldest child of James F and
   Sabrina E Freeman, was born in Rarden, Scioto County,
   Ohio, January 24, 1865   Resides with her parents at
   Wamsley, Ohio

2. Anna Jane Freeman, the second daughter of James F
   and Sabrina E Freeman, was born in Wamsley, Adams
   County, Ohio, February 2, 1868, and died June 16, 1868

3 Icie Pearl Freeman, the third daughter of James F and
   Sabrina E Freeman, was born in Wamsley, Adams County,
   Ohio, November 11, 1878   She was married near Wams-
   ley, Ohio, by the Rev William Hill, March 24, 1897, to
   Samuel Layton, a son of Robert and Sarah R. Layton, he
   having been born in Harrison County, Kentucky, May 25,
   1874 — a farmer — and removed with his parents to Adams
   County, Ohio, in March, 1887   Residence, near Wamsley,
   Ohio   To them was born a son

   I —Denver Freeman Layton, born January 3, 1898.

4 Catherine Bertella Freeman, called "Kate," the fourth
   daughter of James F and Sabrina E. Freeman, was born in
   Wamsley Ohio, January 27, 1881   She was married at the
   residence of her parents in Wamsley, Ohio, by the Rev
   Hiram Runyan, a minister of the C U Church, April 16,
   1898, to James O McCormick, a son of J W and Mary I

McCormick he having been born in Wamsley, Adams
County Ohio, August 25, 1876, and is by occupation a
farmer To them was born a son

I —Leslie Everett McCormick was born at Wamsley, Ohio,
March 10, 1890

VIII —Mary Catherine Freeman, the eighth child and third
daughter of Isme and Susannah Freeman, was born in Scioto
County, Ohio, February 8, 1837, and died November 11, 1839,
aged 2 years, 9 months and 3 days

IX —Nancy Jane Freeman, the ninth child and fourth daughter
of Isme and Susannah Freeman was born in Scioto County,
Ohio, September 27, 1839, and died near Wamsley, Ohio, on
Sunday March 17, 1895, in the 56th year of her age She was
married near Wamsley, Adams County, Ohio, August 18, 1858,
by the Rev Jesse Wamsley, to Moses Wamsley, a son of William and Elizabeth Wamsley, he having been born June 5,
1838 Mr Wamsley is a farmer, and continues to reside near
Wamsley, Adams County, Ohio To them were born seven
children

1 Josephine Wamsley, the eldest child of Moses and N Jane
Wamsley, was born near Wamsley, Ohio, March 1, 1859
She was married by the Rev Jesse Wamsley March 15,
1884, to Arthur Nelson Covert, a son of Larkin N and
Martha Covert, he having been born in Ripley, Brown
County, Ohio, March 25, 1859 He is a farmer by occupa-
tion Residence, near Wamsley, Ohio To them were
born three children

I —Arthur Cloyd Covert, son of Arthur N and Josephine
Covert, was born July 3, 1885

II —Estella Larkin Covert, was born August 23, 1887

III —Izora Violet Covert was born April 8, 1890

2 James Martin Wamsley the second child and eldest son
of Moses and N Jane Wamsley, was born near Wamsley,
Ohio, June 25, 1860 He was married by John P Young,
Esq December 25, 1889, to Mary Jane Montgomery, a
daughter of William H and Mahala Montgomery, she having been born in Rome, Adams County Ohio, November 13,
1861 To them were born two children Residence near
Wamsley, Ohio

I —Pansy Estella Wamsley, daughter of James M and Mary
J Wamsley, was born November 4, 1890

II —Ruth Wamsley was born ———

3 Andrew Crowell Wamsley, the third child and second son
of Moses and N Jane Wamsley, was born near Wamsley,
Ohio, May 18, 1863, and died January 11, 1864

4 Mary Estella Wamsley, the fourth child and second daughter of Moses and N Jane Wamsley, was born near Wamsley, Ohio, April 26, 1866 She was married by the Rev
Jesse Wamsley, December 9, 1886, to William Henry Jones
a son of Andrew J and Jane Jones, he having been born at
White Oak, Adams County, Ohio, May 31, 1859 He is a
practical farmer To them was born one child

I —Flossie Pearl Jones

5 Samuel Kinton Wamsley, the fifth child of Moses and N
Jane Wamsley, was born near Wamsley, Ohio, January 29,
1869 He was married, May 4, 1892, to Dora Montgomery.
To them was born one child

I —Clyde Owen Wamsley, son of Samuel K and Dora
Wamsley, was born in December, 1893

6 Alton Clyde Wamsley, the sixth child and fourth son of
Moses and N. Jane Wamsley, was born near Wamsley,
Ohio, December 24, 1871

7 Chalmers Wiley Wamsley, the seventh child and fifth son of
Moses and N Jane Wamsley, was born near Wamsley,
Ohio, March 2, 1876

X —Joseph Oppy Freeman, the tenth child and sixth son of
Isme and Susannah Freeman, was born in Scioto County,
Ohio, January 13, 1842, and died August 10, 1843, aged 1 year,
6 months and 28 days

XI —Sarah Ellen Freeman, the eleventh child, and fifth daughter
of Isme and Susannah Freeman, was born in Scioto County,
Ohio, May 3, 1844 She was married by the Rev. Mr Middle-
ton, October 8, 1863, to George Marion Wykoff, a son of
James and Rachel Wykoff, he having been born near Wamsley, Adams County, Ohio Sarah Ellen Freeman Wykoff
died October 23, 1887, aged 43 years, 6 months and 15 days
To them were born four children

1 James Marshall Wykoff, the eldest child of George M and Sarah Ellen Wykoff, was born in Adams County Ohio, February 14, 1866 He was married by Henry Hall, Esq , near Jay Bird, Adams County, Ohio, January 5, 1888, to Ann Etta Newman, a daughter of M. H and Sarah Newman. To them was born one child

I —Minnie Marie Wykoff, daughter of James M and Ann E Wykoff, was born in Scioto County, Ohio, March 6, 1889

2 Minnie Estella Wykoff, the second child and only daughter of George M and Sarah E Wykoff, was born in Adams County, Ohio, September 22, 1871 She was married by Henry Hall, Esq , April 29, 1888, to James Renwick Davis, a son of Thomas and Elizabeth Davis, he having been born July 27, 1866 Occupation, a merchant clerk Residence, Rarden, Scioto County, Ohio To them were born two children

I —Dora Edna Davis was born in Rarden, Ohio, January 16, 1889

II —Edith Lucile Davis was born in Rarden, Ohio, March 24, 1891.

3 John Wolf Wykoff, the third child and second son of George M and Sarah E Wykoff was born in Adams County, Ohio, December 22, 1872.

4 William Alfred Wykoff, the fourth child and third son of George M and Sarah Ellen Freeman, Wykoff, was born in Adams County, Ohio, April 5, 1878, and died July 6, 1898, in the 21st year of his age

XII —Moses Edward Freeman, the twelfth child and seventh son of Isme and Susannah Freeman, was born in Brush Creek Township, Scioto County, Ohio, February 26 1847 He removed to the West about 1870 and settled in Iowa Since 1875 he has not been heard from, probably dead.

XIII —Isaac Blair Freeman, the thirteenth child and eighth son of Isme Freeman, the elder child by his second wife, Martha Freeman, was born in Scioto County, Ohio, March 10, 1851, and died July 6 1861, aged 10 years, 3 months and 26 days

XIV —Mary Alice Freeman, the fourteenth child of Isme Freeman, the second child by his second wife, Martha Freeman, was born in Scioto County, Ohio, August 23, 1853, and died August 20, 1861, aged eight years, lacking three days

CHAPTER V

Isaac Freeman, the fifth child and second son of Michael and Elizabeth Duncan Freeman, was born on Blue Creek, in Adams County, Ohio, December 25 1802, and died in his own home, on Jake's Creek, Delaware County, Indiana, January 5, 1864, in the 62d year of his age   He was brought up on his father's farm, on Scioto Brush Creek, in Adams County, Ohio   He was a practical and successful farmer   Isaac Freeman was married near Portsmouth, Scioto County, Ohio, December 26, 1822, to Jemima Moore, a daughter of John and Sarah Moore she having been born in what is now Adams County, Ohio, February 21, 1801, and died at the old home, on Jake's Creek, Delaware County, Indiana, February 15, 1871, where she had lived with her husband and family many years   She survived her husband for several years   She was a faithful and devout member of the Methodist Episcopal Church   Isaac Freeman remained in Adams and Scioto Counties Ohio, about a dozen years after his marriage   About 1834 he removed with his family to Delaware County, Indiana, and purchased a farm on Jake's Creek, four miles north of Muncie, where they continued to reside   He was a prosperous, contented and useful man, although for many years before his death he was afflicted with a peculiar and severe form of indigestion, which made it difficult for him to retain food upon his stomach   Isaac Freeman was of devout spirit, earnest and active in Christian work, and for many years a steward class leader, and local preacher or exhorter, in the Methodist Episcopal Church   Isaac and Jemima Freeman brought up a family of seven children some of whom still survive to revere their memory and call them blessed   Nearly all of them were members of the church of their father and mother, devout in their Christian lives, and blessings to society

I —Sarah Freeman, the eldest child of Isaac and Jemima Freeman, was born in Adams County, Ohio, November 16, 1823,
and died in Eaton, Delaware County, Indiana, June 15, 1878, in
the 55th year of her age   She spent her childhood in Ohio,
and removed with her parents to Delaware County, Indiana,
about 1834, with whom she continued to live. In 1856 she
taught school in Adams County, Ohio, near where she spent
her youthful days   She was married by the Rev Nathaniel
Williams at the home of her uncle, Aaron F Steen, near Mt.
Leigh, Adams County, Ohio, December 24, 1857, to William
Alexander Blair, a son of William L and Catherine E Blair,
he having been born near Winchester, Adams County, Ohio,
April 15, 1832   They resided in Adams County, Ohio, and in
Selma and Eaton in Delaware County, Indiana   W Alexander Blair now resides in Muncie, Indiana   To them were born
three children

  1 Dora Ette Blair, the eldest child of W Alexander and
     Sarah Freeman Blair, was born near Winchester, Adams
     County, Ohio, October 29, 1858   She was married by the
     Rev O M Todd, a Presbyterian clergyman, in Eaton, Indi-
     ana, August 19, 1875, to Zechariah Young, a son of Enoch
     and Catherine A Young, he having been born in Delaware
     County, Indiana, May 6, 1851 — occupation, a merchant
     Residence, Eaton, Delaware County, Indiana   To them
     were born three children

       I —Theodore Ovid Young was born at Eaton, Indiana,
          March 3, 1877, and died at the same place, April 3, 1877

       II —Ralph Blair Young was born at Eaton, Indiana, Febru-
          ary 23, 1891, and died June 9, 1891

       III —Mary Eve Young was born at Eaton, Indiana, July 9,
          1892

  2 Austa Ellen Blair, the second daughter of W Alexander
     and Sarah Freeman Blair, was born near Winchester, Adams
     County, Ohio, February 19, 1860, and died in Milroy, Indi-
     ana, September 4, 1883, in the 24th year of her age   She
     was married at the home of her parents in Eaton, Indiana,
     by the Rev Thomas Sells, a M E minister, in April, 1882,
     to James L Walters, a son of Jacob Walters, he having been
     born in Delaware County, Indiana, and died in Eaton, Indi-
     ana, December 18, 1882

3 Ora Maud Blair the third daughter of W Alexander and
Sarah Freeman Blair was born in Selma, Delaware County,
Indiana, November 7 1868   She was married by the Rev
Frank H Hays a Presbyterian clergyman, in Muncie, Indi-
ana, October 26, 1892, to Irving Allen   Residence, Hart-
ford City, Indiana

II —John Freeman, the second child and eldest son of Isaac and
Jemima Freeman, was born in Adams County, Ohio January
26, 1825   He was taken by his parents to Delaware County,
Indiana, when he was about nine years old, and here he was
brought up on his father's farm, about four miles north of
Muncie, Indiana, situated on Jake's Creek   He was married
in Delaware County, Indiana, by the Rev John B Birt, July
19, 1849 to Mary Jane Wier, a daughter of Thomas and Mary
Wier, she having been born in Delaware County Indiana
Postoffice address, Muncie Indiana   To them were born three
children

   1 James Birt Freeman, the eldest child of John and Mary
   Jane Freeman, was born at their home, near Jake's Creek,
   Delaware County, Indiana, August 21, 1850, and died July
   31 1851

   2 Paulina Jane Freeman the second child and only daughter,
   of John and Mary Jane Freeman was born near Jake's
   Creek, in Delaware County, Indiana January 1 1852   She
   was married at the same place by the Rev Benjamin Smith,
   September 10 1872 to Fernando C Storer a merchant in
   Muncie Indiana, a son of Margaret and Asher Storer he
   having been born in Delaware County Indiana, June 19,
   1850 — members of the Quaker Church   To them were
   born two children

      I —Elizabeth Blanche Storer, the elder daughter of Fer-
      nando C and Paulina Jane Freeman Storer, was born in
      Delaware County, Indiana, April 20 1873

      II —Jessie Pearl Storer the second daughter, was born in
      Delaware County, Indiana September 9 1875

   3 Thomas Jefferson Freeman, the third child and second son
   of John and Mary Jane Freeman was born near Jake's
   Creek, Delaware County, Indiana, November 14, 1858, and
   brought up on his father's farm   He was married by the
   Rev R H Smith, December 20, 1882 to Birdella McColm,

a daughter of Henry A and Harriet McColm, of Delaware
County, Indiana, she having been born in Adams County,
Ohio, May 20, 1862   To them was born one child

1—Oran Freeman, son of Thomas Jefferson and Birdella
Freeman, was born in Delaware County, Indiana, July 10,
1886

III—Mary Jane Freeman, the third child and second daughter
of Isaac and Jemima Freeman, was born in Adams County,
Ohio, July 18, 1828, and was brought by her parents to Delaware County, Indiana when about six years old   She was
married on Jake's Creek, Delaware County, Indiana, April 20,
1852, to Andrew R Hoover, a son of Eli and Margaret Hoover,
he having been born in Delaware County, Indiana   They continued to reside in Delaware County, Indiana, until 1881, when
they removed to Florida and located near Ocala Marion
County, Florida, where they still live   To them were born
seven children

1 Eli Freeman Hoover, the eldest child of Andrew R and
Mary Jane Hoover, was born in Delaware County, Indi-
ana, April 8, 1854   He was married, December 11, 1877, to
Dora Shick

2 John Emery Hoover, the second son of Andrew R and
Mary Jane Hoover, was born in Delaware County, Indiana,
August 23, 1857   He was married, December 8, 1886, to
Alice J. Cook

3 Jemima Arabella Hoover, the third child and eldest daughter of Andrew R and Mary Jane Hoover, was born in Delaware County Indiana, March 8, 1859, and died April 2,
1860

4 Cassius Lemon Hoover, the fourth child and third son of
Andrew R and Mary Jane Hoover, was born in Delaware
County, Indiana, March 23 1860 He was married,
November 28, 1884, to Eveline Sayers

5 Olive Ann Hoover, the fifth child and second daughter of
Andrew R. and Mary Jane Hoover, was born in Delaware
County, Indiana, April 10, 1861, and died January 25, 1864

6 Wilbur Fiske Hoover, the sixth child and fourth son of
Andrew R and Mary Jane Hoover, was born in Delaware

County, Indiana, May 15, 1865   He was married, November 21, 1889 to Flora Helva

7 Lulu Dell Hoover, the seventh child and third daughter of Andrew R and Mary Jane Hoover, was born in Delaware County, Indiana, February 3, 1873

IV —Louisa Freeman, the fourth child and third daughter of Isaac and Jemima Freeman, was born in Scioto County, Ohio, January 18, 1830   She was brought to Delaware County, Indiana, when she was a little child, and brought up on her father's farm   She died in Adams County, Indiana, January 20, 1877, aged 47 years and 2 days   She was married at the home of her parents, on Jake's Creek, Delaware County, Indiana, by the Rev Benjamin Smith, January 15, 1861, to James Wesley Jones, a son of William and Elizabeth Jones, he having been born in Rockingham County, Virginia, in 1836. Family residence, Willshire, Van Wert County Ohio   To them were born nine children

1 Jemima A Jones, the eldest child of J Wesley and Louisa Freeman Jones, was born in Delaware County Indiana, December 14, 1861.   She was married in Adams County, Indiana, to John M Allspaw, a son of Robert and Margaret E Allspaw, he having been born in Adams County, Indiana Residence, Bluffton, Indiana   To them were born four children

   I —Blanche Allspaw, the eldest child of John M and Jemima A Allspaw, was born in Willshire, Van Wert County, Ohio November 15, 1882.

   II —Charles Floyd Allspaw was born in New Carlisle, Clarke County Ohio, September 14, 1884, and died March 14 1885

   III —Cecil Allspaw as born in Van Wert County, Ohio, September 15, 1885.

   IV —Harry Allspaw was born in Willshire Van Wert County, Ohio, July 9, 1887

2 William J Jones, the second child and eldest son of J Wesley and Louisa Freeman Jones was born in Delaware County Indiana, January 31, 1862, and died March 1, 1862

3. 4 5 Triplets, two boys and a girl, children of J Wesley and Louisa Freeman Jones. were born in Delaware County, Indiana. September 5. 1862, and died the same day.

6 James Lewis Freeman Jones, the sixth child and fourth son of J Wesley and Louisa Freeman Jones, was born in Delaware County, Indiana, July 26, 1864   Residence, Palo, Linn County, Iowa

7 John A Jones, the seventh child and fifth son of J Wesley and Louisa Freeman Jones. was born in Delaware County, Indiana, March 1, 1867   He was married by Samuel McClintock, May 10, 1893, to Nora Mather she having been born January 20 1873   Residence, Palo, Linn County, Iowa

8 Mary E Jones the eighth child and third daughter of J Wesley and Louisa Freeman Jones, was born in Delaware County, Indiana, February 8, 1868, and died August 3, 1877

9 Margaret M Jones, the ninth child and fourth daughter of J Wesley and Louisa Freeman Jones, was born in Adams County Indiana, May 1, 1872, and died August 31, 1877

V —Emily Pilcher Freeman, the fifth child and fourth daughter of Isaac and Jemima Freeman, was born in Scioto County, Ohio, February 12, 1832, and was brought by her parents to Delaware County, Indiana. when a little child, and grew up to womanhood on her father's farm on Jake's Creek four miles north of Muncie Delaware County. Indiana   She died in Muncie. Indiana, February 27, 1890, aged 58 years and 15 days   Emily Pilcher Freeman was married at the home of her parents. in 1858, to David Hoover, a son of Eli and Margaret Hoover. he having been born in Delaware County Indiana, and died June 7, 1881.   He kept a meat market in Muncie, Indiana   To them was born one child

1 Charles Sumner Hoover, son of David and Emily P Hoover was born on Jake's Creek, in Delaware County. Indiana, in 1859, and died in Muncie, Indiana, in 1882, aged 23 years

VI —Elizabeth Ann Freeman, the sixth child and fifth daughter of Isaac and Jemima Freeman, was born on the old home farm on Jake's Creek, Delaware County, Indiana, July 13, 1839 She was married by Samuel McClintock, Esq, May 13 1873.

to Levi Denny Lewis, a son of John and Elizabeth Denny
Lewis, he having been born in Guernsey County, Ohio, June
28, 1829 Residence, Mt Vernon, Iowa John Lewis, the
father of Levi D Lewis, was born in Pennsylvania, September
12, 1794, was married to Elizabeth Denny, March 6 1821, she
having been born in New Jersey, November 2, 1801 To Levi
D and Elizabeth Ann Freeman Lewis were born two children

1 Nellie Lewis, the elder child of Levi Denny and Elizabeth
Ann Freeman Lewis was born August 29, 1874, and died
the same day.

2. John Freeman Lewis, the second child of Levi Denny and
Elizabeth Ann Freeman Lewis, was born in Delaware
County, Indiana November 27, 1876 Residence, Spring-
port, Henry County, Indiana

VII —William Freeman, the seventh child and second son of
Isaac and Jemima Freeman, was born on the old home farm
on Jake s Creek, Delaware County, Indiana, October 14, 1837,
and was brought up on the farm He is by trade a carpenter
He was married by the Rev Benjamin Smith, in Delaware
County, Indiana, September 26, 1860, to Nancy Catherine
Munsey, a daughter of Skidmore and Maria Munsey, she hav-
ing been born in Delaware County, Indiana Residence,
Eaton, Delaware County, Indiana To them were born three
children

1 Laura Belle Freeman, the eldest child of William and
Nancy C Freeman was born in Delaware County, Indiana,
August 24, 1862, and died August 11, 1865

2 Charles Skidmore Freeman, the second child and only son
of William and Nancy C Freeman, was born in Delaware
County, Indiana, October 21, 1868 Residence Eaton,
Indiana

3 Dottie Dell Freeman, the third child, the second and only
daughter now living, of William and Nancy C Freeman,
was born in Delaware County, Indiana July 19, 1878. Residence, Eaton, Indiana

VIII —James Lewis Freeman the eighth child and third son
of Isaac and Jemima Freeman, was born on the old home
farm on Jake's Creek, in Delaware County, Indiana, Septem-

ber 21, 1844, and there grew up to manhood and assisted on
the farm until his father's death   He was married by the Rev
S H Brooks, in Muncie, Indiana, December 20. 1864, to Mary
Frances Walling. a daughter of Thomas and Susannah Walling, she having been born August 8, 1843   James L Freeman
is a prosperous farmer   He and his wife are faithful members
of the Society of Friends, or what is usually called the Quaker
Church   Their post-office address is Springport, Henry
County, Indiana   To them were born five children

1 Carl Volney Freeman, the eldest child of James L and
   Mary F Freeman, was born in Delaware County, Indiana,
   June 12, 1869

2 Susan Freeman, the second child and elder daughter of
   James L and Mary F Freeman, was born in Delaware
   County, Indiana, January 8, 1871, and died September 7,
   1871

3 Mark Huber Freeman, the third child and second son of
   James L and Mary F Freeman, was born in Delaware
   County, Indiana, April 6, 1872

4 Joseph Emery Freeman, the fourth child and third son of
   James L and Mary F Freeman, was born in Delaware
   County, Indiana, December 18, 1874

5 Nellie Emeline Freeman, the fifth child, the youngest, a
   daughter of James Lewis and Mary Frances Freeman, was
   born in Delaware County, Indiana, November 17, 1876

CHAPTER VI

James Freeman, the sixth child and third son of Michael and
Elizabeth Duncan Freeman was born on Blue Creek, in Adams
County, Ohio June 12 1805, and died on his own farm, two miles
east of the mouth of Blue Creek, February 18, 1860, in the 55th
year of his age   James Freeman was brought up on his father's
farm, and for many years he lived on a farm adjoining that of
the old home. on the east fork of Scioto Brush Creek, near its
source, and about ten miles east of West Union. Ohio on the

main road leading to Portsmouth He was by occupation a shoemaker, and an excellent workman at his trade He also superintended the work on his farm, notwithstanding a lameness in one of his legs In the year 1852 he purchased from J M. Walden a fine farm of 300 acres on the east fork of Scioto Brush Creek, about two miles below the mouth of Blue Creek, in Adams County, Ohio This place was about fifteen miles east of West Union, on the main road, and twenty miles west from Portsmouth It was also about eleven miles by way of the Blue Creek Road to Rome, a village on the Ohio River, which was his principal business or trading point James Freeman was a man of genial nature, kind-hearted ard social, an agreeable companion, delighting in society, ever ready to confer a favor and well respected by all who knew him He was married near West Union, Ohio, January 29, 1829, to Ann Prather, a daughter of John and Elizabeth Wilson Prather, she having been born near West Union, Ohio, June 15, 1808, and died at her pleasant home, January 28, 1870, in the 62d year of her age, beloved by all who knew her. John Prather and Elizabeth Wilson Prather, the father and mother of Ann Prather Freeman, were brought up on the eastern shore of Maryland, and were married in Queen Anne County, Maryland near where Moses and Nancy Freeman first settled in America They removed to the Northwest Territory and settled in what is now Adams County, Ohio, about the same time, and probably came in the same company of emigrants to the West with Michael and Joseph Freeman and their families John and Elizabeth Wilson Prather were the parents of two sons and eleven daughters, all of whom were married and had families of their own To James and Ann Prather Freeman were born four children

I —George Marion Freeman, the eldest child of James and Ann Prather Freeman, was born in Jefferson Township, Adams County, Ohio, about two miles west of the mouth of Blue Creek, December 18, 1829 George M Freeman was an influential citizen, was frequently elected a Justice of the Peace, and was universally respected He was never married, and was for many years manager of the old home farm He died at the old home farm of his father and mother two miles below the mouth of Blue Creek, in Adams County, Ohio January 29, 1891, aged 61 years 1 month and 11 days

II—Levi Freeman, the second son of James and Ann Prather
Freeman was born near Blue Creek, in Jefferson Township,
Adams County, Ohio, September 14, 1832, and died at his own
home, only a few miles from the same place, May 11, 1868, in
the 36th year of his age He was by occupation a farmer and
resided upon an excellent farm, adjoining that of his father.
Levi Freeman was married by Henry Prather Esq , near West
Union, Adams County, Ohio, October 25, 1854, to Narcissus
Smalley a daughter of Abraham and Elizabeth Smalley, she
having been born October 9, 1831 She was also a granddaughter of John and Mary Williams, who was formerly Mary
Duncan, a sister of Elizabeth Duncan, who married Michael
Freeman, in Maryland It is probable also that John and
Mary Duncan Williams came from Maryland to the Northwest Territory at the same time and in the same company of
emigrants to the West with Michael and Joseph Freeman, and
John Prather and their young families, but that John Williams
and his family first settled in Kentucky They afterwards
located in Adams County, Ohio Thus it appears that Levi
Freeman's grandmother and his wife's grandmother, were sis-
ters, and that they themselves were second cousins To them
was born one child

   1. Volney Wilson Freeman, a son of Levi and Narcissus Smalley Freeman, was born near Blue Creek Adams County,
Ohio, October 26, 1855 He lives upon his mother's farm,
and has full charge of all business matters He is the only
heir to the estate He was married in Portsmouth, Ohio,
by Rev David S Tappan November 26 1894, to Anna Cora
Ham, a daughter of Clark and Martha W Ham They have
no children His post-office address is Blue Creek Ohio

III—John Prather Freeman, the third son of James and Ann
Prather Freeman, was born near Blue Creek, in Jefferson
Township, Adams County, Ohio July 5, 1838 He was by
occupation a farmer, and resided upon his father's farm two
miles below Blue Creek, on the east fork of Scioto Brush
Creek He was married by the Rev Jesse Wamsley September
18 1861 to Belle Elliott a daughter of John and Elizabeth
Elliott Less than four months after his marriage John P
Freeman suddenly sickened and died from typhoid fever, at
the old home, where both his parents died, January 9 1862, in
the 24th year of his age No children.

IV—Wilson Shannon Freeman, the fourth son of James and Ann Prather Freeman, was born near Blue Creek, in Jefferson Township, Adams County, Ohio, November 21, 1840 and was brought up on his father's farm. He is a successful farmer and prosperous in business. He was always fond of the chase, delighting very much in the fox chase or deer hunt, and usually returned with good success. He is a fine marksman—almost a sure-shot—and woe to the animal that comes within the range of his trusty rifle. When just a young boy of perhaps a dozen years, he quite surprised his father and older brothers by coming home hurriedly and saying that he had killed a deer while he was out looking for squirrels. They could hardly believe the report, but followed him to the place and found the deer dead, its throat neatly cut with his pocket knife. The fatal bullet from his squirrel rifle had entered its heart. During the winter season he delights to spend a few weeks in some remote locality looking for game, and seldom returns home empty-handed. One season he went far down the Ohio and Mississippi Rivers into Arkansas and secured a large amount of game. W Shannon Freeman was married by the Rev Jesse Wamsley, at the residence of the bride's parents, one mile from his father's house, September 18, 1862, to Rebecca Ann Bradley, a daughter of James Madison and Eliza Peters Bradley, she having been born August 12, 1839, and died at the family home, March 19, 1891, in the 52d year of her age. After his marriage, W Shannon Freeman lived in the old family home of his parents, on the East Fork of Scioto Brush Creek two miles below Blue Creek, a happy life of more than twenty-eight years before his wife's death. He has no children. His present post-office address is Wamsley, Adams County, Ohio.

CHAPTER VII

Moses Freeman, the seventh child and fourth son of Michael and Elizabeth Duncan Freeman, was born on Blue Creek, in Adams County, Ohio, February 10, 1808, and was brought up on his father's farm. He was married by the Rev James Smith, near Jacktown Ohio, January 13, 1831, to Margaret McCormick a daughter of James and Hannah McCormick, she having been born September 4. 1811, and died in Otway, Scioto County Ohio, March 12, 1900 in the 89th year of her age   After a long happy, and useful Christian life, her mortal remains were lovingly borne to the White Oak cemetery, and laid by the side of her husband After his marriage he purchased a farm and located upon it near the mouth of the west fork of Scioto Brush Creek, in Scioto County, Ohio   Upon this farm the village of Otway was afterwards built and near by the old home is the railway station of the Cincinnati, Portsmouth & Virginia Railroad   At this place Moses Freeman lived happily and prosperously with his family until his death, August 10, 1851, in the 44th year of his age He was a devout and earnest Christian man, of excellent spirit a member of the M E Church, and so also was his excellent wife and so his children afterwards became all being highly esteemed and greatly respected   To Moses and Margaret McCormick Freeman were born four children

I —Mary Jane Freeman, the eldest child of Moses and Margaret McCormick Freeman, was born at Otway, Scioto County Ohio, January 4 1832 and died in Otway, Ohio   She grew up to womanhood on her father's farm   She was married by the Rev Jesse Wamsley, March 25 1849, at Otway, Ohio to Joseph W Tracy — a farmer — a son of Jonathan and Elizabeth Tracy, he having been born near Otway, O , and died at Mt Pleasant, Iowa   To them were born four children

  1   Elizabeth M Tracy, the eldest child of Joseph W and Mary Jane Freeman Tracy, was born at Henly, Ohio, January 1, 1850, and died at Mt Pleasant, Iowa

  2   Emma A Tracy, the second daughter of Joseph W and Mary J Tracy was born at Henly, Ohio, March 20, 1852, and died at the same place, May 18, 1857

  3   James F Tracy, the third child and elder son of Joseph W and Mary Jane Tracy, was born at Henly, Ohio April 23, 1854, and died May 28, 1857

  4   Moses William Tracy the fourth child and second son of Joseph W and Mary J Tracy, was born at Henly, Scioto County Ohio August 18, 1856 and died at Mt Pleasant, Henry County Iowa, September 24, 1865, aged 9 years

II —James Gavitt Freeman, the second child and only son of Moses and Margaret McCormick Freeman, was born on his father's farm where the village of Otway now stands, in Scioto

County, Ohio, March 3, 1835 Here he was brought up He
has followed the profession of a teacher, and a successful business man He has frequently been elected a Justice of the
Peace, entire confidence being placed in his judgment and
integrity He is an earnest and faithful Christian man, and
brought up his family in the M E and C U Churches He
was married by the Rev Jesse Wamsley, near Otway, Scioto
County, Ohio, September 11, 1856, to Millie Eliza Tracy, a
daughter of Jonathan and Elizabeth Tracy, she having been
born in Adams County, Ohio, July 1, 1834, and died from
pneumonia at Otway, Scioto County, Ohio, February 21, 1899,
in the 65th year of her age Her body was tenderly laid away
to rest in the Otway cemetery Residence Otway, Ohio To
them were born five children

1 Moses Franklin Freeman, the eldest child of James G and
   Millie E Freeman, was born near Otway, Scioto County,
   Ohio, April 22, 1861, and died February 2, 1863, in the sec-
   ond year of his age

2 James Watson Freeman, the second son of James G and
   Millie E Freeman, was born near Otway, Scioto County,
   Ohio, June 27, 1864 He was married by Joseph Ashton
   Esq, at Portsmouth, Scioto County, Ohio, September 8,
   1886, to Harriet Eliza Dear, a daughter of Albert and Mar-
   garet Dear Residence, Nocatee, De Soto County, Florida

3 Edwin Jonathan Freeman, the third son of James G and
   Millie E Freeman, was born near Otway, Ohio June 30,
   1868, and died April 15, 1870, in the second year of his age

4 William Milton Freeman, the fourth son of James G and
   Millie E Freeman, was born near Otway, Ohio May 6
   1871 He was married by the Rev William Hill, near Blue
   Creek, Adams County, Ohio, October 5, 1890, to Jennie
   Humble, a daughter of Elias and Margaret Humble she
   having been born in Adams County, Ohio

5 Joseph Alva Freeman, the fifth son of James G and Millie
   E Freeman, was born in Otway, Scioto County Ohio, July
   1, 1873, and died July 26, 1896, aged 23 years and 25 days

III—Elizabeth Hannah Freeman, the third child and second
   daughter of Moses and Margaret McCormick Freeman, was
   born at the home of her parents, on the farm where the village
   of Otway, Scioto County, Ohio, now stands, October 17, 1840
   She was married by the Rev Jesse Wamsley, in Otway, Ohio,

April 12 1863, to Thomas Hart Benton Jones, a son of Andrew Bird and Vienna Jones, he having been born on his father's farm, four miles west of Otway, Ohio, March 5 1838 He resides with his family upon the farm on which he was born — a practical farmer To them were born six children Residence, near Otway, Scioto County, Ohio

1 Emma Estella Jones, the eldest child of Thomas Hart Benton and Elizabeth Hannah Freeman Jones, was born near Otway Scioto County Ohio, January 5, 1864

2 James Mockley Jones, the second child and eldest son of Thomas H B and Elizabeth Hannah Jones, was born near Otway, Ohio, August 1, 1865 He was married near Mineral Springs, Ohio, March 5, 1891, to Martha A Liston, a daughter of Francis M and Sarah C Liston she having been born near Mineral Springs, Adams County, Ohio, December 29, 1869

3 Bertha Ethel Jones, the third child and second daughter of Thomas H. B and Elizabeth Hannah Jones, was born near Otway, Ohio, March 24, 1872 She was married near Otway, Ohio, October 26, 1890, to William E Brown, a son of James G and Almedith Brown, he having been born in Scioto County, Ohio, August 12 1871 To them one child was born

> 1 —Grace Myrtle Brown, a daughter of William E and Bertha Ethel Brown, was born August 29, 1891

4 Thomas Carey Jones, the fourth child and second son of Thomas H. B and Elizabeth Hannah Jones, was born near Otway, Ohio, June 16, 1874

5 Edwin Watson Jones, the fifth child and third son of Thomas H B and Elizabeth Hannah Jones, was born near Otway Ohio, January 2, 1878   ,

6 Alva Burton Jones, the sixth child and fourth son of Thomas H B and Elizabeth Hannah Jones, was born near Otway, Scioto County, Ohio, April 6, 1882

IV —Sarah Emeline Freeman, the fourth child and third daughter of Moses and Margaret McCormick Freeman, was born on her father's farm, where now stands the village of Otway, Scioto County, Ohio, October 16 1847, and died in Otway, Ohio, May 30, 1891 in the 44th year of her age She was married by the Rev Jesse Wamsley, in Otway, Ohio, Octo-

ber 15, 1872, to Joseph McDowell Reynolds — a farmer of
Peebles, Ohio — a son of Oliver and Zylpha Reynolds, he
having been born in Brown County, Ohio, July 14, 1842 To
them were born three children

1 Oscar Freeman Reynolds, the eldest child of Joseph M and
Sarah Emeline Freeman Reynolds, was born May 8 1874

2 Jesse Truman Reynolds, the second son of Joseph M and
Sarah Emeline Reynolds, was born June 3, 1876

3 Maud Reynolds, the third child and only daughter of Joseph
M and Sarah Emeline Reynolds, was born August 19 1884,
and died near Otway, Ohio, October 26, 1892, in the 9th
year of her age

CHAPTER VIII

Mary Freeman, the eighth child and fourth daughter of
Michael and Elizabeth Duncan Freeman, was born on the old
 Freeman farm, on the east fork of Scioto Brush Creek, two
miles west of Blue Creek, Adams County, Ohio, October 7, 1810,
and died in Knoxville, Tennessee, July 27, 1895, at 6 30 A M, in
the 85th year of her age Her body was tenderly laid away to
rest in the beautiful Woodlawn cemetery, near Xenia Ohio
Mary Freeman was brought up in her father's family, early gave
her heart to Christ, and united with the Methodist Episcopal
Church at the residence of Josiah Williams, on Blue Creek, when
about thirteen years old, and ever afterwards maintained a consistent and devoted religious life She was married at the
residence of her parents, on the old Freeman farm, on Scioto
Brush Creek, two miles west of Blue Creek, Adams County, Ohio,
March 25 1830 to Aaron Faris Steen, a son of Alexander and
Agnes Nancy Steen, he having been born near Flemingsburgh,
Kentucky, August 23, 1807, and died at his residence, near
Xenia, Ohio, February 15, 1881, in the 74th year of his age His
body was buried in the beautiful Woodlawn cemetery near that
city At the time of the marriage of Mary Freeman to Aaron F
Steen, the streams were so swollen by the heavy rains that had
prevailed for several days previous, that the minister who was to

have married them — the Rev John Meek — failed to reach the
place and the ceremony was performed by John Williams, Esq,
a Justice of the Peace, who was present as an invited guest   After
her marriage she removed with her husband to a farm which he
had leased for five years   It was situated on Brush Creek, at the
mouth of Elk Run, two miles from Winchester, Ohio, and about
the same distance from the Mt Leigh Presbyterian Church, with
which they soon became connected, and were regular in their
attendance   In the fall of 1834, the lease having nearly expired,
at the earnest request of her parents, they returned to live with
them in their old age on the old home farm on Scioto Brush
Creek, she to care for the family, and her husband to take charge
of the farm and manage the business   The following spring,
April 14, 1835 her father, Michael Freeman died, but she and her
husband continued to live there for thirteen years and have
charge of affairs as before, during which time they were members
and attendants of the Presbyterian Church at West Union, Ohio
In the autumn of 1848 she removed with her husband and family
to a farm he had purchased near Mt Leigh, two miles from
Youngsville, and three miles from Winchester, Adams County,
Ohio bringing her mother and eldest sister to make their permanent home with them   Here they connected themselves again
with the Mt Leigh Presbyterian Church of which, the next year
Mr Steen was ordained a ruling elder, and continued such until
his removal from the place   The children were all baptized in
this church and regular attendants   In the summer of 1865
Mr Steen sold his farm near Mt. Leigh and purchased a tract
of eleven acres of land adjoining the city of Xenia, Ohio to which
they removed the same season and where they continued to
reside   Here they united with the First Presbyterian Church in
Xenia, under the pastorate of the Rev William T Findley, D D
The fiftieth anniversary of the marriage of Aaron F and Mary
Freeman Steen was appropriately celebrated at their residence,
near Xenia, Ohio, March 25, 1880   It was a delightful occasion,
which but seldom occurs   All their living children and grand-
children were present with but a single exception, together with
many friends and relatives, including Mrs Catherine E Blair, a
sister of Mr Steen, and who was present at the wedding fifty
years before   Dr John A Steen, of Ripley, Ohio, presented his
uncle with a gold-headed cane   Several short addresses were
made, a number of presents given, an elegant dinner served, a
very enjoyable social gathering, and the whole concluded with

religious services   Less than a year after this golden wedding, February 15, 1881 Aaron F Steen died, and his body was lovingly laid away in Woodlawn cemetery   After her husband s death, Mrs Steen and her daughter moved into Xenia and lived together until the latter's marriage, in 1885, then for two years in Yellow Springs, Ohio, and from 1887 until her death in 1895, at the home ot her son, Prof E Watson Steen in Knoxville, Tennessee   During this time, however she made extensive visits to her daughter, who lived at Westboro Massachusetts, and afterwards at Cincinnati, Ohio   While residing at Knoxville she was a member of the Third Presbyterian Church (Southern), in which she delighted to worship   Mary Freeman Steen was devotedly attached to her children and faithful in religious instruction and Christian training   She was permitted to see the fruit of her labors, all ot them being brought into the kingdom   Well does the writer remember how she used to take him to some private chamber alone, or under some tree in the orchard, and talk to him earnestly and lovingly atter he had been guilty of wrong-doing, and with tears in her eyes kneel down and pray to God for his pardon and grace to make him a better boy   God was pleased to bless her instructions and prayers to his conversion, and to the life work of a Christian minister   She was one of God s noble women, whose influence was not only exerted at home, but whose power for good was recognized wherever she was known   She was noted for her generous hospitality her genial social nature kindness of heart, and benevolent disposition ever ready to make sacrifices for the good of others   She died at the ripe old age of nearly 85 years, in the full hope of a glorious immortality   She was the mother of nine children

I —Wilson Freeman Steen the eldest child of Aaron F and Mary Freeman Steen, was born on the farm, two miles east of Winchester, Adams County, Ohio May 11, 1831 and died in Xenia Ohio, March 20, 1882 aged 51 years, 10 months and 9 days   He was brought up on his father's farm, where he worked in summer and attended school in winter   When he became of age he spent a winter in Delaware County, Indiana, where he taught school   In 1853 he returned to Adams County, Ohio, and engaged in teaching near the place of his birth   When a youth he was a regular attendant at church and a diligent student in the Sabbath-school an energetic and industrious young man   He early gave his heart to Christ and

united with the Mt Leigh Presbyterian Church on profession
cf faith, in 1849, maintaining ever afterwards a devout, consistent and useful Christian life   He was always fond of music, and,
like his father and grandfather   had a natural talent for it
After a special course of study at the Musical Normal School,
he became a teacher of vocal and instrumental music   He
taught very many classes in Adams, Brown, and Clermont
Counties, often as many of three or four upon each secular day
of the week   In 1860 he removed to Xenia, Ohio, where he
followed his chosen profession until 1867 when he removed to
Cincinnati, and in addition to his music classes he opened a
store for the sale of musical instruments   In 1867 he removed to
Ludlow, Kentucky, just across the river, but continued his
business in Cincinnati, as before   Here himself and family
connected themselves with the First Presbyterian Church of
which his brother was pastor   He was elected ordained and
installed a ruling elder in this church September 15, 1878, in
which position he became an efficient officer and a very useful
man   He was possessed of a kind heart, gentle spirit, and was
interested in every good work   As leader of the music and
teacher in the Sabbath-school his labors were exceedingly
profitable   In the autumn of 1882, owing to failing health, he
was obliged to quit his business.   He returned to Xenia, Ohio
to spend his last days, but continued very meek, patient, and
uncomplaining to the very last   He died, March 20 1883 in
the sure and certain hope of a blessed inheritance, a man greatly
beloved by all who knew him   His body was laid away in
Woodlawn cemetery near Xenia, Ohio   W Freeman Steen
was married by the Rev William Fee, in Xenia, Ohio, December 25, 1862, to Emma Marie Stipp, a daughter of Dr Nathan
B and Eliza J Stipp, she having been born in Bellebrook,
Greene County Ohio, October 8 1842, and died in Cincinnati,
Ohio October 3, 1899   To them were born three children

1 Edith Marie Steen, the eldest child and only daughter of W
   Freeman and Emma M Steen, was born in Xenia, Ohio
   March 28, 1864, and was brought up in her father's family
   She was married in Cincinnati, Ohio, by the Rev Edward
   Anderson, September 17, 1882 (?), to Charles William
   Bogart the only child of John H and Anna M Bogart he
   having been born in Ludlow, Kentucky, April 20 1864
   They have resided in Ludlow, Kentucky, Cincinnati, Ohio,
   Covington, Kentucky, and Hamilton, Ohio   Charles Wil-

ham Bogart is a fine musician, an excellent wood engraver,
and a skillful machinist — manufacturer of gas engines
Residence, Buffalo, New York To them were born six
children

I—Charles Franklin Bogart, the eldest son of C William
and Edith M Steen Bogart was born in Cincinnati, Ohio
July 12, 1883

II—Edwin Richard Bogart, the second son of C William
and Edith M Steen Bogart, was born in Ludlow, Kentucky December 28, 1885

III—John Albert Bogart, the third son of C William and
Edith M Steen Bogart, was born in Ludlow, Kentucky
February 18, 1889

IV—James Helmus Bogart, the fourth son of C William
and Edith M Steen Bogart was born in Ludlow, Kentucky August 26 1891

V—Lawrence Wilson Bogart, the fifth son of C William
and Edith M Steen Bogart was born in Covington Kentucky February 2, 1894

VI—Marine Dewey Bogart, the fifth son of C William and
Edith M Steen Bogart was born in Hamilton Ohio,
January 30, 1898

2 Earnest Linden Steen, the second child and elder son of
W Freeman and Emma M Steen, was born in Xenia Ohio,
November 2 1865 He resided with his parents until his
father s death, and afterwards in Cincinnati, Ohio He died
in Cincinnati, Ohio, July 8, 1894, aged 28 years 8 months
and 6 days

3 Clarence Freeman Steen, the third and youngest child of
W Freeman and Emma M Steen was born in Ludlow, Kentucky, February 23 1879 After his father's death he resided
with his mother until 1890 then spent four years with his
uncle, Prof F Watson Steen, at Knoxville Tennessee,
attending school In 1894 he returned to Cincinnati, Ohio,
where he learned his trade, and resided with his mother until
her death Clarence F Steen is a bookbinder by trade
Residence Toledo, Ohio

II—Eli Watson Steen the second son of Aaron F and Mary
Freeman Steen was born at the home of his parents, on Brush
Creek, near the mouth of Elk Run, two miles east of Winches-

ter, Adams County, Ohio, August 6, 1833 When less than two
years of age he was taken by his parents to the old Freeman
farm, on Scioto Brush Creek, two miles west of Blue Creek,
and ten miles east of West Union, where his happy boyhood
days were spent, attending school and assisting his father on
the farm He removed again with his parents, August 31,
1848, to the farm his father had purchased, near Mt Leigh,
and about a mile from the place where he was born, and where
he assisted his father until he became of age He was a regular attendant at the Mt Leigh Church and Sabbath-school for
many years, early gave his heart to Christ, and united with the
church in 1849, and ever afterwards maintained a consistent
Christian life He was very fond of music, and, like his
brother, father and grandfather possessed a talent for it
After he became of age he pursued musical studies in Normal
musical schools in Russellville and Decatur, Ohio under the
direction of Prof D H Baldwin He afterwards became a
proficient and popular teacher of vocal and instrumental music
Sometimes he would have charge of two or three classes in
different parts of the country on each secular day of the week
He possessed a sweet voice, was a fine singer, and to some
extent a composer of music His services were eagerly sought
for musical institutes, conventions and as an instructor in
Normal music classes, in which he was eminently successful
In the summer of 1862 he enlisted in the army as a private in
Company E, Ninety-first Regiment Ohio Volunteer Infantry
was promoted to Second Sergeant, on a few occasions acted as
Captain, and was stationed principally in West Virginia
Owing to the failure of health, he was honorably discharged
from the service in 1864 In 1867 he sold his farm near Mt
Leigh and removed to Xenia, Ohio and continued to follow his
profession for several years He then became a traveling agent
for the music house of D H Baldwin & Co of Cincinnati
For several years he was in very poor health, unable to attend
to business, and living at Xenia, Ohio In May, 1880 he
removed to Knoxville, Tennessee, and in connection with
another gentleman opened a music house under the firm name
of "Steen & Marshall" but in a year or two dissolved the part-
nership and continued in business by himself alone After the
death of his father he was made executor of his estate In
1887 his mother came to reside in his family, where she
remained until her death, in 1895 but she spent a considerable

part of the time with her daughter, at Westboro, Massachusetts,
and in Cincinnati, Ohio   Prof E Watson Steen was married
by the Rev James Dunlap, in West Union Adams County,
Ohio October 25, 1855, to Julia Emily Lilly Diboll, a daughter of Dr Victor M and Philena L Diboll, she having been
born near Sardinia, Brown County, Ohio, December 7, 1839,
and died at their pleasant home, in Knoxville, Tennessee, September 17, 1896, in the 57th year of her age   Her body was
interred in the beautiful Woodlawn cemetery, near Xenia, Ohio,
September 19, 1896   To them were born three children.
Family residence, 19 Pearl Place, Knoxville, Tennessee   After
their removal to Knoxville, Prof E Watson Steen, his wife,
daughter and mother all united with the Third Presbyterian
Church (Southern), in which he was duly elected ordained,
and installed a ruling elder, which office he still holds

1   Laura Alice Steen, the eldest daughter of Prof E Watson
    and Julia E L Steen was born at the home of her parents,
    on the farm near Mt Leigh and Youngsville, Adams County,
    Ohio, August 18, 1856, and continued to reside with her
    parents there until their removal to Xenia, Ohio, in 1867,
    when she was about eleven years old   At Xenia she early
    united with the First Presbyterian Church, and maintained
    a consistent Christian life   Here also she obtained a good
    English education in the Xenia schools   Like her father,
    she possessed splendid musical talents, which were culti-
    vated to a high degree, so that she became not only an accom-
    plished singer, but an excellent teacher of instrumental
    music as well   Miss L Allie Steen was a young lady of
    good social qualities and attractive manner, but alas her
    genial and useful career was soon cut off by that dread dis-
    ease quick consumption, from which she died at the home
    of her parents in Xenia, Ohio, June 5 1878, in the 22d year
    of her age and in the certain hope of a blessed immortality
    Her funeral took place from the Presbyterian Church and
    her body was laid away to rest in the beautiful Woodlawn
    cemetery, near Xenia Ohio

2   Mary Estella Steen the second daughter of Professor E
    Watson and Julia E L Steen, was born at the home of her
    parents, on the farm near Mt Leigh and Youngsville, Adams
    County Ohio January 13, 1860   She was brought by her
    parents to Xenia, Ohio, in 1867, when she was a little girl
    seven years of age, where she was brought up and educated

She early united with the First Presbyterian Church in Xenia, and maintained a consistent Christian life She secured a good English education in the Xenia schools, and was an interesting and accomplished young lady, possessing considerable literary talent She published several interesting original stories of high merit, one of which was entitled Book Learning vs Housekeeping " Mary E Steen was married by her uncle, the Rev Moses D A Steen, at the Grand Hotel, in Cincinnati, Ohio, March 16 1880, to Earnest L Lawrence, of Xenia, Ohio   After their marriage they resided in Xenia for about five years, where Mr Lawrence was agent for the Xenia Powder Company   In 1885 they removed to Chicago, Illinois where they continued till her death, March 19, 1890 at the age of 30 years, 2 months and 6 days   Her body was interred in Chicago, Illinois   To them were born two children

I —Mildred Lawrence the eldest child of Earnest L and Mary E Steen Lawrence, was born in Xenia, Ohio, June 1, 1884   Residence, Chicago, Illinois

II —Meredith Fay Lawrence, the second child of Earnest L and Mary E Steen Lawrence was born in Chicago, Illinois, November 10, 1889   Residence, Chicago, Illinois

3. Julia Emerine Pearl Steen the third and youngest daughter of Prof E Watson and Julia E L Steen, was born at the home of her parents in Xenia, Greene County, Ohio, August 8, 1871, where she resided until 1880, when she was brought by her parents to Knoxville, Tennessee   Here she received a good English education, and became an attractive and accomplished young lady   She is possessed of fine musical talents, which, under her father's direction, have been cultivated to a very high degree   She is not only a cultivated classical, and very popular singer, but an excellent instrumental performer in public as well   She has composed and published many pieces which are quite meritorious She took the first prize offered by the Atlanta Constitution for the best musical composition, open to the musicians of several States besides other prizes J E Pearl Steen was married at Knoxville Tennessee, December 4, 1899 to Dr Charles A Garratt   Residence Knoxville, Tennessee

III —Samuel Martin Steen, the third son of Aaron F and Mary Freeman Steen, was born on the old Freeman homestead on the east fork of Scioto Brush Creek, two miles above the mouth of Blue Creek, and ten miles east of West Union, in Adams County, Ohio, July 5, 1836. Here he continued until he was twelve years of age, going to school and assisting his father as he was able. In 1848 he removed with the family to their new home, on his father's farm, twenty miles distant, near Mt. Leigh, Adams County, Ohio, where he continued to work on the farm in summer and go to school in winter. He was also a regular attendant at the Mt. Leigh Church and Sabbath-school. Having secured a good common school education at Mt. Leigh, he afterwards attended the State Normal School at Lebanon Ohio, under the direction of Prof. E. H. Holbrook, and became a teacher. S. Martin Steen was a young man of brilliant talents, a natural mathematician, delighting in difficult problems. He was also able in argument, and extremely fond of it. Often he would present a proposition to his brother or other friend to see which side he would take, then take the opposite and use such strong arguments as to compel his opponent to admit that he was wrong. Then, taking a good hearty laugh, he would take up the other side of the question and convince him back again that he was right after all, and enjoy another hearty laugh. He had the peculiar faculty of doing this without giving offense, and purely from the love of debate. He was a young man of great energy and perseverance, and had his life been spared, he would probably have made his mark in the world. He taught quite successfully several terms of school, the last one being at Sandy Springs Ohio, near the Ohio River, which closed in June, 1859. While living here he united with the Methodist Episcopal Church upon profession of faith in Christ. Here also, while engaged in teaching, he caught a very severe cold, which settled upon his lungs and developed into quick consumption. S. Martin Steen died at the residence of his parents near Mt. Leigh, Adams County, Ohio, with an assured hope of a glorious immortality October 13, 1859, aged 23 years 3 months, and 8 days. His body was laid away to rest in the Mt. Leigh cemetery.

IV—John Truman Steen, the fourth son of Aaron F. and Mary Freeman Steen, was born at the old Freeman homestead on Scioto Brush Creek, in Jefferson Township Adams County Ohio, May 18, 1838. His earliest associations were thus connected with the home of his mother's parents, who came from Maryland into that locality in 1797 and where his mother was

born and brought up When a little child he went to school
on Blue Creek, two and one-half miles away, near the mouth
of which beautiful stream there was a junction of the roads
leading to Portsmouth, Rome, and West Union There was
also a post-office, country store and blacksmith shop where
the local business was principally transacted In 1848, when
ten years of age, he was taken by his parents to their new home
on the farm his father had purchased, three miles from Winchester, on the road leading to Mt Leigh, where he grew to
manhood In the Mt Leigh school he secured a good common English education, afterwards attended the State Normal
School at Lebanon, Ohio and qualified himself for a teacher, in
which profession he was especially successful He was exceedingly fond of music, and is said to have had the finest and most
natural talent for it of any member of the family His social
qualities were also of a high order and his company was sought
and enjoyed by all his acquaintances   J Truman Steen united
with the Mt Leigh Presbyterian Church on profession of faith
in Christ, June 9 1858, and continued to be an earnest, devoted
and useful Christian While engaged in teaching school at
Harsha's Mills, he caught a very severe cold, which developed
into consumption He died at his father s residence, universally beloved and greatly lamented, June 25, 1862, aged 24
years 1 month and 7 days His body was lovingly laid away
to rest in the cemetery at Mt Leigh, Adams County Ohio

V —Moses Duncan Alexander Steen, the fifth son of Aaron F
and Mary Freeman Steen was born at the old Freeman home,
on Scioto Brush Creek, two miles west of Blue Creek, and ten
miles east of West Union, Ohio, April 24, 1841 His earliest
recollections were of the old house in which he and also his
mother were born, the orchard, the creek, rocky cliffs and cedar
trees, the high bridge, the sugar camp, the old church grave-
yard, and the surrounding hills The death of his little brother
in the autumn of 1844 was never effaced from his memory
His first day at school on Blue Creek remains as a vivid picture,
one brother holding each hand as they walked along until they
came to Smalley's store, where they bought a "primer' with
bright pictures, and proceeded to the school-house, where the
teacher took him on her lap The school exhibition which
occurred later on, at which he recited "Twinkle twinkle little
star " and the long Sabbath services of the Seceders, at Waite's
Mill have never been forgotten He was taken by his parents

to their new home, near Mt Leigh, August 31, 1848, was baptized in the Mt Leigh Presbyterian Church by the Rev James
Dunlap together with each of his elder brothers, October 2,
1848 He was afterwards a regular attendant at the church,
Sabbath-school, and district school, and Sabbath afternoons
were devoted by his parents to the religious instruction of their
children Moses D A Steen united with the Mt Leigh Presbyterian Church on profession of faith, June 8, 1858, and began
a course of study in North Liberty Academy, afterwards spent
three years in Salem Academy, under Rev Dr James A I
Lowes, one year in Hanover College, and completed his classical course in Miami University, Oxford, Ohio, from which he
graduated, receiving the degree of B A, June 27, 1866 He
entered the United Presbyterian Theological Seminary at
Xenia, Ohio, September 1, 1866 where he spent one term He
afterwards attended the Presbyterian Theological Seminary of
the Northwest at Chicago, Illinois from which he graduated
April 1, 1869 having spent the autumn session of 1868 in the
Theological Seminary at Princeton, New Jersey He was
licensed to preach the Gospel in Hillsboro, Ohio by the O S
Presbytery, of Chillicothe April 8, 1868, and spent the summer months in preaching in Mt Sterling and Sharpsburgh,
Kentucky Immediately after his graduation from the Theological Seminary in April 1869, he took charge of the church
in Worthington near Columbus, Ohio The next year he
accepted an invitation to the church in Vevay Indiana and in
that church was ordained to the ministry by the Presbytery of
New Albany, September 8, 1870 In January 1872, he
accepted a call to the pastorate at Solon, near Cleveland Ohio,
which he resigned in April 1873, to accept a call to Conneautville, Pennsylvania, which church he resigned in December,
1874, and took charge of the church at Waterford Pennsylvania In May, 1875 he accepted a call to Ludlow Kentucky,
opposite Cincinnati, Ohio where he remained six years and
three months Through his patient and persistent labors a
heavy and pressing mortgage debt was removed, and the
church placed upon a substantial basis of prosperity In the
summer of 1877 while in charge of this church he made an
extensive journey through Europe, traveling in Ireland, Scotland, England Holland, Belgium Germany Switzerland and
France, and returned to his work with renewed vigor He
resigned his church at Ludlow, Kentucky, to accept an invita-

tion to the church at Pleasant Ridge, a suburb of Cincinnati,
Ohio and the next season he accepted an invitation to Davis-
ville, California, and entered upon his work September 1 1882,
but a few months later returned East and supplied the churches
of Troy and Edwardsville, Illinois   October 1, 1883, he
accepted an invitation to Tabernacle Church Gunnison Colorado   The next year he went to Black Hawk Colorado   In
1885 he went to the Pacific Coast supplied the First Church,
Tacoma, Washington, a few weeks and then the Snohomish
Church, Washington, for one year the church doubling its
membership during that time   In July 1886 he accepted
an invitation to the church at Woodbridge, California to begin
his labors September 1, 1886, where he was afterwards installed
pastor, and where he still remains   Moses D A Steen and his
wife have devoted their leisure hours to special courses of study
together, receiving diplomas from the C L S C in 1889 and
afterwards the Guild of the Seven Seals   They completed the
Bible Correspondence School Course of seven years and
received their diplomas in 1890   In connection with his work
in Woodbridge, California, Dr Steen organized a Presbyterian
church at Clements, fourteen miles distant where no church
of any denomination had existed before, September 29 1889
and supplied it at regular intervals for several years   With a
membership of only nine persons he was instrumental in building and dedicating without debt, on this mission field, a beautiful and substantial church edifice worth $5,000   In 1888 he
was invited by the faculty to preach the annual sermon at San
Joaquin Valley College   and a few days later at the annual
meeting of the Board of Trustees they conferred upon him the
honorary degree of Doctor of Divinity   In 1889 the University of Wooster conferred upon him the degree of Doctor of
Philosophy upon thesis and examination   The twenty-fifth
anniversary, or silver wedding of Rev Dr and Mrs M D A
Steen was appropriately celebrated in the church at Woodbridge, California, under the auspices of 'The King's Daughters," and was a most delightful occasion   Dr Steen has frequently been chosen Moderator of the Presbytery with which he
was connected, and since 1893 has been the Stated Clerk and
Treasurer of the Presbytery of Stockton   He was chosen
Commissioner to the Presbyterian General Assemblies at Madison, Wisconsin, in 1880   at Omaha, Nebraska in 1887   at
Saratoga Springs, New York in 1894   In 1895 he was chosen

by the General Assembly at Pittsburgh, Pennsylvania a dele-
gate to the ' Council of Reformed Churches throughout the
world, holding the Presbyterian system,' to meet in Glasgow,
Scotland, in 1896   On this occasion he was accompanied by
his wife, and after the Council they extended their journeys
throughout British and Continental Europe, returning to
America by way of the Northern Route, by the Coast of Lab-
rador, through the Strait of Belle Isle the Gulf and River of
St Lawrence to Quebec, and Montreal   He has traveled
extensively in the United States the Provinces of Canada and
Mexico   Including missionary work in the West with other
journeys, he has visited every State and Territory in the American Union except Alaska, and preached the Gospel in many of
them — in the forest, in log cabins in frontier settlements in
school-houses, on river and ocean steamers, in village and city
churches, among Indians, Mexicans, and all classes and con-
ditions of people rich and poor, learned and illiterate   Rev
Moses D A Steen was married by the Rev William R Par-
sons, at the home of the bride's parents, in Worthington near
Columbus, Ohio June 22 1870, to Mary Foster a daughter of
Archibald and Harriet Foster formerly of Sugar Creek,
Venango County, Pennsylvania she having been born at Sugar
Creek, Pennsylvania, July 21 1843   She united with the Sugar
Creek Presbyterian Church upon profession of faith June 8,
1858, and is an amiable devout, and useful Christian   To
them was born one child   Residence, Woodbridge, California

1 Lulu Grace Steen, the only child of Rev Moses D A and
   Mary Foster Steen, was born in Conneautville Pennsylvania
   July 4, 1873 and died in Ludlow, Kentucky July 3, 1876
   aged three years   She was a general favorite a remarkably
   bright and interesting child, affectionate obedient patient,
   and yet full of life and enthusiasm   She was intelligent
   beyond her years and devotional to an eminent degree   On
   her third birthday, July 4 1876 the centennial of American
   independence, her mortal remains were laid away to rest in
   the beautiful Woodlawn cemetery near Xenia, Ohio

VI —Josiah James Steen, the sixth son of Aaron F and Mary
   Freeman Steen, was born on the old Freeman farm, on Scioto
   Brush Creek, two miles west of Blue Creek, in Adams County
   Ohio, February 25, 1844 and died September 8, 1844 aged 8
   months and 13 days   His body was laid away in the Blue

Creek cemetery "A sweet little bud taken from earth to bloom in heaven "

VII—Sarah Catherine Steen called "Kate, the seventh child and only daughter of Aaron F and Mary Freeman Steen, was born at the home of her parents, near Mt Leigh, and three miles east of Winchester Adams County, Ohio April 1, 1853 She continued to reside with her parents on the farm, near Mt Leigh and Winchester, Ohio and attended the public school the church and the Sabbath-school at Mt Leigh until she was twelve years of age when she removed with her parents to their new home at Xenia Ohio where she was brought up and educated She graduated from the Xenia High School in 1872, and in early life united with the First Presbyterian Church of that city Like her father and elder brothers she possessed fine musical talents, which she delighted to cultivate and exercise, and under the instruction of skillful teachers she soon acquired a cultivated voice, skill in execution, and became an accomplished teacher of vocal and instrumental music In 1879 she taught for six months in Clarksville Tennessee After the death of her father, in 1881, she and her mother moved into the heart of the city where they lived together, and she taught music privately to many pupils In 1883 she accepted the position of teacher of vocal music and voice culture in Antioch College, Yellow Springs, Ohio, still making her home with her mother in Xenia until after her marriage S Kate Steen was married by the Rev John S Axtell, in Xenia, Ohio, December 24, 1885, to the Rev Elijah Alfred Coil, and January 1, 1886, they removed to Yellow Springs Ohio, taking her mother with them The Rev E Alfred Coil was a son of Jesse A and Lydia Coil, and was born May 2, 1858, and brought up on his father's farm, near Delphos, Allen County, Ohio His mother died when he was a little child only five years old He attended school in the neighborhood and secured his higher education at Antioch College, Yellow Springs, Ohio, where, as his music teacher he became acquainted with his future wife He accepted a call to the pastorate of the Christian Church at Yellow Springs Ohio, September 1, 1885, and continued in charge two years Then September 1, 1887, he accepted a call to the First Unitarian Church in Westboro, Worcester County Massachusetts, where he remained in charge four years Then again he removed to Cincinnati Ohio September 1, 1891, and became pastor of

the Unity Church of that city, where he remained four years,
until September 1, 1895, when he accepted a call to the pastorate of the First Unitarian Church of Marietta, Ohio where he
is still in charge To them were born four children Residence, Marietta, Ohio

1 Emery Wilbur Coil, the eldest child of the Rev L Alfred
and Kate Steen Coil, was born in Westboro Massachusetts
in Worcester County, about thirty miles from Boston September 28, 1888

2 Harold Coil, the second son of the Rev E Alfred and Kate
Steen Coil, was born in Westboro, Worcester County, Massachusetts, May 1, 1891

3 Alfreda Coil, the third child and only daughter of the Rev
E Alfred and Kate Steen Coil, was born in Cincinnati, Ohio,
June 15, 1892

4 Marion Coil, the fourth child and third son of the Rev E
Alfred and Kate Steen Coil, was born in Marietta, Ohio,
November 30, 1895

VIII —Isaac Birt Steen the eighth child and seventh son of
Aaron F and Mary Freeman Steen, was born near Mt Leigh
and three miles east of Winchester Adams County Ohio June
8, 1856, and died June 16, 1856 aged 8 days

IX —William Wirt Steen the ninth child and eighth son of
Aaron Faris and Mary Freeman Steen was born on the farm,
near Mt Leigh, and three miles east of Winchester Adams
County, Ohio June 8, 1856, and died June 26 1856 aged 18
days The two last named were twin brothers, and were buried
in the same grave, in the Mt Leigh cemetery

CHAPTER IX

Charles Freeman, the ninth child and fifth son of Michael
and Elizabeth Duncan Freeman was born on the old Freeman
farm, on Scioto Brush Creek, the east fork, near its source, two
miles west of the mouth of Blue Creek, and about ten miles east
of West Union, Adams County, Ohio, February 12, 1813, and
died at his own home, in the Greenbrier neighborhood, about two

miles from his father s farm, in December, 1843, after suffering several weeks from the effects of a fall, injuring his spine Charles Freeman was brought up on his father's farm, and was a practical farmer himself at the time of his death, aged about 30 years and 10 months Charles Freeman was married near the ford of Ohio Brush Creek, east of West Union Ohio, in March 1831, to Keziah Osman, a daughter of John and Hannah Carson Osman, she having been born July 19 1815, and died in Delaware County, Indiana, many years after the death of her husband To them were born four children

I—Matilda Ann Freeman, the eldest child of Charles and Keziah Osman Freeman was born in Greenbrier neighborhood three miles west of the mouth of Blue Creek in Adams County, Ohio, October 9, 1836, and died at her home, near Rome, Adams County, Ohio, a village on the Ohio River, January 20, 1875 in the 39th year of her age She was married by Laban Parks Esq , in Adams County, Ohio, January 19, 1854, to Allen Trimble Cox — a farmer — a son of Allen Trimble and Mary Cox, he having been born in Adams County, Ohio, April 10, 1832 To them were born eleven children They lived near Rome, Adams County Ohio, (Stout's P O)

1 Albert Collins Cox the eldest child of Allen T and Matilda Ann Freeman Cox, was born near Rome Adams County Ohio, December 20 1854, and died October 24, 1871, in the 17th year of his age

2 Samantha Alice Cox, the second child and eldest daughter of Allen T and Matilda Ann Freeman Cox, was born near Rome, Adams County, Ohio, October 16, 1857 She was married, December 4, 1873, to Christopher Columbus Mason, he having been born June 22, 1855, by whom she had nine children Residence, near Rome, Stout s Post-office, Adams County, Ohio

    I—Sarah Ann Mason, the eldest child of Christopher Columbus and Samantha Alice Mason, was born July 4 1874

    II—Elgia Ellen Mason, the second child of C C and Samantha A Mason, was born September 23, 1876

    III—Maggie May Mason, the third daughter of C C and S A Mason was born September 16, 1878

    IV—James Allen Mason the fourth child and eldest son of C C and S A Mason, was born November 15, 1881

V —Mattie Mariah Mason, the fifth child and fourth daughter of C C. and S A Mason, was born February 11, 1884

VI —Charles William Mason, the sixth child and second son of C C and S A Mason, was born September 16, 1886, and died November 29, 1886

VII —Wheeler Leroy Mason, the seventh child and third son of C C. and S. A Mason, was born October 16 1887, and died August 27, 1888

VIII —Infant son the eighth child of C C and S A Mason, was born and died July 17, 1889

IX —Chester Columbus Mason the ninth child and fifth son of Christopher Columbus and Samantha Alice Mason, was born July 16, 1891

3 Mary Keziah Cox, the third child and second daughter of Allen T and Matilda Ann Freeman Cox was born near Rome, Adams County, Ohio, December 22, 1859 She was married, December 23, 1877, to Scott H McGovney, he having been born December 18, 1856 To them were born five children Residence near Rome, Stout's Post-office, Adams County, Ohio

1 —Alexander H McGovney, the eldest child of Scott H and Mary K McGovney, was born November 27, 1878

II —Albertine McGovney, the second child and eldest daughter of Scott H and Mary K McGovney, was born August 15, 1880

III —Annie McGovney, the third child and second daughter of Scott H and Mary K McGovney, was born August 11, 1882

IV —William Scott McGovney, the fourth child and second son of Scott H and Mary K McGovney, was born October 22, 1886

V —Mary Alice McGovney, the fifth child and third daughter of Scott H and Mary K McGovney, was born January 23, 1891

4 Martha Mariah Cox, the fourth child and third daughter of Allen T and Matilda Ann Freeman Cox, was born near Rome, Stout's Post-office, Adams County Ohio December 22, 1859 a twin sister of Mary Keziah Cox She was married, February 11, 1877, to James William Mason, he having

been born October 29, 1854   To them were born seven children   Residence, Pond Run, Scioto County, Ohio

I —Everett Wilson Mason, the eldest child of James William and Martha Mariah Mason was born November 2, 1877

II —Elva May Mason the second child and eldest daughter of James William and Martha Mariah Mason, was born July 31, 1879.

III —Esta Florence Mason, the third child and second daughter of James W and Martha M Mason, was born September 17, 1880

IV —Arthur Crayton Mason, the fourth child and second son of James W and Martha M Mason, was born June 29, 1882

V —Katie Ann Mason, the fifth child and third daughter of James W and Martha M Mason, was born March 4, 1884

VI —Charles William Mason, the sixth child and third son of James W and Martha M Mason, was born September 26, 1886

VII —Allen Corwin Mason, the seventh child and fourth son of James W and Martha M Mason, was born September 10, 1888

5   Elizabeth Albertine Cox, the fifth child and fourth daughter of Allen T. and Matilda Ann Freeman Cox was born near Rome, Stout's Post-office, Adams County, Ohio, February 24, 1863   She was married, December 1, 1880, to George Leonard Franz he having been born October 19, 1858   To them were born five children   Residence, Selig, Adams County, Ohio

I —Maud Franz the eldest child of George Leonard and Elizabeth Albertine Franz, was born April 23, 1881 and died April 24, 1881.

II —Minnie Jane Franz, the second daughter of George L and E Albertine Franz was born November 25, 1882

III —Essie May Franz, the third daughter of George L and E Albertine Franz, was born April 26, 1884

IV —William Robert Franz the fourth child and only son of George L and E Albertine Franz was born November 12, 1885

1ʳ Ida Florence Franz, the fifth child and fourth daughter of George Leonard, and Elizabeth Albertine Franz, was born July 25, 1888

6 Charles Marion Cox, the sixth child and second son of Allen T and Matilda Ann Freeman Cox, was born near Rome, Stout's Post-office, Adams County, Ohio, May 17, 1865 He was married, April 15, 1890, to Elizabeth Newman, she having been born December 15 1869 Residence, near Rome, Stout's Post-office, Adams County, Ohio

7 Willis Freeman Cox, the seventh child and third son of Allen T and Matilda Ann Freeman Cox, was born near Rome, Adams County Ohio, October 1, 1866, and died November 13, 1868, aged 2 years, 1 month and 13 days

8. John Sherman Cox, the eighth child and fourth son of Allen T and Matilda Ann Freeman Cox, a twin brother of Andrew Sheridan Cox, was born near Rome, Stout s Post-office, Adams County, Ohio, December 13, 1868

9 Andrew Sheridan Cox the ninth child and fifth son of Allen T and Matilda Ann Freeman Cox, a twin brother of John Sherman Cox, was born near Rome, Stout's Post-office, Adams County, Ohio, December 13, 1868

10 Alfred Nelson Cox, the tenth child and sixth son of Allen T and Matilda Ann Freeman Cox, was born near Rome, Stout's Post-office, Adams County, Ohio, November 9 1872

11 Minnie Jane Cox, the eleventh child and fifth daughter of Allen Trimble and Matilda Ann Freeman Cox, was born near Rome, Stout's Post-office, Adams County, Ohio, April 3, 1874 She was married by the Rev. J W Shumaker, at West Union, Adams County, Ohio, December 21, 1893, to John C Harris, he having been born in Carter County, Kentucky April 20 1854, to whom was born one child

1—Elsie Inez Harris, a daughter of John C and Minnie Jane Harris, was born January 23, 1895

II—John Jasper Freeman the second child and only son of Charles and Keziah Osman Freeman, was born in Greenbrier neighborhood, three miles west of the mouth of Blue Creek, in Adams County, Ohio, September 20 1838, and died near Muncie, Delaware County Indiana, September 11 1882, in the 44th year of his age J Jasper Freeman was married in Delaware County, Indiana, November 10 1859, to Mary M Scudder, a daughter of ———— and Jane Scudder, she having been born September 5 1840 To them were born two children Family residence, near Muncie Delaware County, Indiana

1 Charles H Freeman the elder son of J Jasper and Mary M Freeman, was born near Muncie, Delaware County, Indiana, August 4 1860 and died October 5, 1865, aged 5 years 2 months and 1 day

2 John W Freeman the second son of J Jasper and Mary M Freeman, was born near Muncie, Delaware County, Indiana, March 16 1863 He was married in Muncie, Indiana December 26 1884, to Ettie J Hardister, who died March 25, 1889 John W Freeman was married a second time, at Point Pleasant Missouri December 25, 1891 to Ida J Shirley and died in Missouri To John W Freeman and his first wife were born two children

   I—Albert R Freeman, the elder child and only son of John W and Ettie J Hardister Freeman, was born near Muncie, Delaware County, Indiana, about 1886

   II—Mabel B Freeman the second child and only daughter of John W and Ettie J Hardister Freeman was born near Muncie Delaware County Indiana about 1889

III—Mary Jane Freeman, the third child and second daughter of Charles and Keziah Osman Freeman, was born in Greenbrier neighborhood, in Jefferson Township Adams County, Ohio, about three miles west of the mouth of Blue Creek, July 29 1842 where she was brought up This was not far from the old Freeman farm, on Scioto Brush Creek where her father was born and brought up She was married by the Rev Samuel Snodgrass, near Muncie, Delaware County, Indiana, April 10, 1863, to Harvey Fodge, he having been born July 1, 1840 They have no children Residence Gaston Delaware County, Indiana

IV—Sarah Mariah Keziah Fear Freeman the fourth and youngest child, and the third daughter of Charles and Keziah Osman Freeman, was born in the Greenbrier neighborhood, in Jefferson Township, Adams County Ohio about three miles west of the mouth of Blue Creek, and not far from her grandfather's (Michael Freeman) farm June 8 1844, and died near Rome Adams County Ohio, (Stout's Post-office,) March 29 1862, aged 17 years 9 months and 21 days Sarah M K F Free-

man was born after the death of her father and brought up in
the family of her uncle and aunt, Aaron F and Mary Freeman
Steen, three miles east of Winchester, Adams County, Ohio,
and near Mt Leigh, where she attended church, Sabbath-
school, and the district school. She was married at the residence of her sister, Matilda Ann, near Rome Adams County
Ohio (Stout's Post-office) by Esquire Cook, March 29, 1860
before she was sixteen years old, to Samuel Ashbury Montgomery a son of Samuel and Huldah Montgomery he having
been born near Rome, Stout's Post-office, Adams County
Ohio August 11, 1830   To them was born one child

1 Alice Belle Montgomery the only child of Samuel Ashbury
   and Sarah Mariah Keziah Fear Freeman Montgomery, was
   born near Rome, Adams County, Ohio, (Stout's Post-office)
   January 13 1861, in which locality she grew up to womanhood She united with the Christian Union Church, in
   Wamsley, Adams County, Ohio in 1882 and has maintained
   a devout Christian character She was married by Jonathan Tracy, Jr Esq, near Rome, Adams County, Ohio,
   (Stout's Post-office,) August 12, 1877 to John Cedar Stout,
   a son of Obadiah and Jane Stout, he having been born near
   Rome, Adams County, Ohio, (Stout's Post-office,) January
   26, 1832, and was by occupation a miller and merchant
   There were no children to this marriage She was married a
   second time by the Rev J E Bailey, in Jeffersonville, Fayette County, Ohio, June 8, 1894, to Franklin Geneva Myers
   he having been born near Portsmouth, Scioto County Ohio,
   May 6 1858 Mr Myers is a member of the Methodist
   Protestant Church, and by occupation a carpenter, builder,
   and contractor Residence Jeffersonville Fayette County,
   Ohio

BOOK TWO.

***

THE DESCENDANTS OF JOSEPH FREEMAN

Joseph Freeman was the second son of Moses and Nancy Knight Freeman, and was born in Queen Anne County, Maryland on the eastern shore of the Chesapeake Bay, about 1768 was married to Elizabeth Higgins about 1795, and removed to the Northwest Territory with his family and friends, in company of emigrants to the far West in 1797, and brought up a family of five children in Adams County, Ohio

***

Joseph Freeman, the second son of Moses and Nancy Knight Freeman, was born near Queenstown, on the eastern shore of the Chesapeake Bay, in Queen Anne County, Maryland, about 1768, and was brought up on his father's farm   He lived in that locality until he was nearly thirty years of age   He was married in Queen Anne County, Maryland, about 1795, to Elizabeth Higgins who was born and brought up in the same locality   In the summer of 1797, in company with his brother Michael Freeman and family, and a goodly number of other emigrants to the far West they left the home of their childhood, bid farewell to dear friends never expecting to see them again, and journeyed along the eastern shore of the Chesapeake Bay, in a northeasterly direction then along the valley of the Susquehanna River, until they reached the Allegheny Mountains, which were crossed with difficulty thence down the Monongahela River to Pittsburgh   From this point they came down the Ohio River on flatboats and landed at a place near the mouth of Ohio Brush Creek, in what was then the great Northwest Territory, thence they journeyed inland, and Joseph Freeman located on lands near the Scioto Brush Creek, east fork, in what is now Adams County, Ohio,

where he continued to reside until his death This settlement
was made when the Northwest Territory was indeed a very new
country, less than ten years after the first permanent white settlement had been made in what is now the great State of Ohio
Here Joseph and Elizabeth Higgins Freeman brought up a family
of five children

CHAPTER I

Nancy Freeman, the eldest child of Joseph and Elizabeth
Higgins Freeman, was born in the great Northwestern Territory,
about 1800, and brought up at the home of her parents on a farm
in Adams County Ohio She was married to Joseph Fry To
them were born three children, as follows

I —Elizabeth Ann Fry
II —Joseph Fry.
III —Louisa Fry

CHAPTER II

Mary Freeman the second daughter of Joseph and Elizabeth
Higgins Freeman, was born on her fathers farm, in Adams
County, Ohio, about 1803, where she grew to womanhood She
was married to Isaac Wamsley To them were born two chil-
dren, as follows·
I —Matilda Wamsley
II —Elizabeth Wamsley

CHAPTER III

William Freeman the third child and eldest son of Joseph and Elizabeth Higgins Freeman, was born in Adams County, Ohio about 1805, and brought up on his father's farm He was a farmer, and lived near the west fork of Scioto Brush Creek not far from the old Ohio Brush Creek iron furnace He was married to Tamar Beach, and brought up his family on the old farm To them were born five children, as follows

I —Joseph Freeman, who married and brought up a family

II —Elias Freeman, who married and brought up a family

III —Sarah Ann Freeman, who was married and brought up a family

IV.—Elizabeth Freeman, who was married and brought up a family

V.—Stephen Freeman, who married and brought up a family

CHAPTER IV

Milby Freeman, the fourth child and second son of Joseph and Elizabeth Higgins Freeman, was born in Adams County, Ohio, June 24 1808, and died at his own home, on a farm adjoining that of his father's old home March 25, 1864 in the 54th year of his age He was a farmer, and brought up his family in the Methodist Episcopal Church Milby Freeman was married in Adams County, Ohio, May 31 1827, to Elizabeth McCormick, a daughter of James and Hannah McCormick, she having been born October 31, 1809 To them were born four children, as follows

I —Sarah Jane Freeman, the eldest child of Milby and Elizabeth McCormick Freeman, was born in Adams County Ohio September 16, 1828, and brought up on her father's farm and died

July 23 1869, in the 41st year of her age She was married at the home of her parents by the Rev Jesse Wamsley, June 13, 1849, to William McCall, he having been born in Scioto County Ohio, July 6, 1819, and died October 14 1891, in the 73d year of his age To them were born ten children, as follows

1 Elizabeth Alice McCall, the eldest child of William and Sarah Jane Freeman McCall, was born in Adams County, Ohio, June 7, 1850 She was married by the Rev Jesse Wamsley, September 9 1875, to Allen Trimble Freeland Residence, Mineral Springs Ohio

2 Ann Medora McCall the second daughter of William and Sarah Jane Freeman McCall, was born in Adams County, Ohio May 16 1852, and died May 11, 1879, in the 27th year of her age

3 Delila Jane McCall, the third daughter of William and Sarah Jane Freeman McCall was born in Adams County, Ohio, December 20 1853 She was married by Sumner Jones, Esq, about 1893, to Joseph McDowell Reynolds formerly a farmer living near Peebles Ohio and whose first wife was Sarah Emeline Freeman, a daughter of Moses and Margaret McCormick Freeman, of Otway Ohio Joseph M Reynolds was a son of Oliver and Zylpha Reynolds, and was born in Brown County Ohio July 14 1842 Residence, Otway Scioto County, Ohio

4 William Franklin McCall, the fourth child and elder son of William and Sarah Jane Freeman McCall was born in Adams County, Ohio April 9 1856 He was married by the Rev Jesse Wamsley, April 28, 1875 to Harriet Elizabeth Suttle Residence, Cedar Mills Adams County Ohio

5 Mary Amanda McCall, the fifth child and fourth daughter of William and Sarah Jane Freeman McCall was born in Adams County, Ohio, August 15 1858 She was married, June 14 1882, to James Monroe Bennington Residence, Cedar Mills Adams County, Ohio

6 James Uriah McCall, the sixth child and second son of William and Sarah Jane Freeman McCall was born in Adams County Ohio, February 28 1860 He was married, Decem-

ber 23 1887, to Anna Patterson   Residence Russell Kentucky

7   Sarah Ella McCall the seventh child and fifth daughter of William and Sarah Jane Freeman McCall, was born in Adams County, Ohio, January 18 1862   She was married January 22 1882, to Christian Henry Ryan   Residence, Mound City Missouri

8   Louisa Addie McCall, the eighth child and sixth daughter of William and Sarah Jane Freeman McCall was born in Adams County Ohio, February 13 1864   Residence Cedar Mills. Adams County, Ohio

9   Emma Isabel McCall, the ninth child and seventh daughter of William and Sarah Jane Freeman McCall, was born in Adams County, Ohio, January 15, 1866 and died August 6, 1867 in the second year of her age

10   Laura Marie McCall, the tenth child and eighth daughter of William and Sarah Jane Freeman McCall was born in Adams County Ohio, February 13 1868, and died March 24, 1869 aged 1 year 1 month and 11 days

II —Nancy Ann Freeman, the second daughter of Milby and Elizabeth McCormick Freeman was born in Adams County, Ohio, December 15, 1831, and brought up on her father's farm   She was married and brought up a family

III —William H Freeman the third child and elder son of Milby and Elizabeth McCormick Freeman was born in Adams County, Ohio, November 27, 1833 and brought up on his father's farm   He was married, and brought up a family Residence, Cedar Mills, Adams County, Ohio

IV —Joseph James Freeman, the fourth child and second son of Milby and Elizabeth McCormick Freeman, was born in Adams County, Ohio November 20, 1841 and was brought up on his father's farm   He is by occupation a farmer, and lives near the old home of his parents   He was married and brought up a family   Residence, Cedar Mills, Adams County, Ohio

CHAPTER V

Sarah Freeman, the fifth and youngest child, the third daughter of Joseph and Elizabeth Higgins Freeman, was born upon her father's farm in Adams County, Ohio, about 1811, where she grew to womanhood. She was married first, to a Mr Jones, who died without children. She was married a second time to a Mr Purnell, by whom she had one child.

I.—A son of —— and Sarah Freeman Purnell was born in Adams County, Ohio.

GENERAL INDEX.

Allen, Ora Maud Blair — One V 1 3
Allen, Irving — One
Allspaw, Jemima A Jones — One V 4 1
Allspaw, John M — One
Allspaw, Blanche — One, V 4 1 1
Allspaw, Charles F — One, V 4 1 2
Allspaw, Cecil — One, V 4 1 3
Allspaw, Harry — One V 4 1 4
Anderson, Huldah Freeman — One II.
Anderson, George — One
Anderson, Elizabeth — One II 1
Anderson, Dycie — One, II 2
Anderson, Sarah — One, II 3
Anderson, Nathaniel — One II 4
Anderson, Catherine — One II 5
Anderson, Paulina — One II 6
Anderson, George F — One II 7

Bennington, Mary A McCall — Two, IV 1 5
Bennington, James M — Two
Blair, Sarah Freeman — One, V 1
Blair, W Alexander — One
Bogart, Edith M Steen — One, VIII 1 1
Bogart, C William — One
Bogart, Charles F — One, VIII 1 1 1
Bogart, Edwin R — One, VIII 1 1 2
Bogart, John A — One VIII 1 1 3
Bogart, James H — One VIII 1 1 4
Bogart, Lawrence W — One, VIII 1 1 5
Bogart, Marine D .. — One, VIII 1 1 6

Coil, S Kate Steen — One VIII 7
Coil, E Alfred — One
Coil, Emery W — One VIII 7 1
Coil, Harold — One VIII 7 2
Coil, Alfred — One VIII 7 3
Coil, Marion — One, VIII 7 4
Covert, Josephine Wamsley — One, IV 9 1
Covert, Arthur N — One
Covert, Arthur C — One IV 9 1 1
Covert, Estella L — One IV 9 1 2
Covert, Izora V — One IV 9 1 3
Cox, Matilda A Freeman — One, IX 1
Cox, Allen T — One
Cox, Albert C — One IX 1 1
Cox, Charles M — One, IX 1 6
Cox, Elizabeth Newman — One
Cox, Willis F — One IX 1 7
Cox, John S — One, IX 1 8
Cox, Andrew S — One IX 1 9
Cox, Alfred N — One, IX 1 10

Davis, Laura B Freeman — One IV 4 8
Davis, Hugh G — One
Davis, Margaret A Freeman — One IV 4 10
Davis, John H — One
Davis, Minnie L Wykoff — One, IV 9 2
Davis, James R — One
Davis, Dora F — One IV 9 2 1
Davis, Edith L — One IV 9 2 2

Dodge, Mary J Freeman — One, IX 3
Dodge, Harvey — One
Franz, Elizabeth A Cox — One, IX 1 5
Franz, George I — One
Franz, Maud — One, IX 1 5 1
Franz, Minnie J — One, IX 1 5 2
Franz, Elsie M — One IX 1 5 3
Franz, William R — One, IX 1 5 4
Franz, Ida F — One IX 1 5 5
Freeland, Elizabeth A McCall — Two IV 1 1
Freeland, Allen T — Two
Freeman, Moses
Freeman, Nancy Knight
Freeman, Nancy
Freeman, John
Freeman, Michael — One
Freeman, Elizabeth Duncan — One
Freeman, Nancy Knight — One I
Freeman, Isme — One, IV
Freeman, Susannah Oppy — One
Freeman, Martha Blair Thompson — One
Freeman, Elizabeth — One IV 1
Freeman, Michael — One IV 2
Freeman, Amanda Thompson — One
Freeman, Sarah Johnson Newland — One
Freeman, Washington — One IV 2 2
Freeman, George P — One, IV 2 3
Freeman, Mary Ann — One, IV 2 4
Freeman, James R — One, IV 2 5
Freeman, Elizabeth A Thompson — One
Freeman, Alpheus D — One IV 2 5 1
Freeman, Vernon F — One IV 2 5 2
Freeman, Ivy L — One, IV 2 5 3
Freeman, Michael D — One, IV 2 5 4
Freeman, John C — One IV 2 5 5
Freeman, W Buchanan — One IV 2 5 6
Freeman, Charles L — One, IV 2 5 7
Freeman, Ida Windle — One
Freeman, Isme W — One IV 2 7
Freeman, Buchanan — One IV 2 8
Freeman, Julia — One IV 2 9
Freeman, Charles S — One IV 2 10
Freeman, Mary D Stiers — One
Freeman, Clovis C — One, IV 2 10 2
Freeman, William A — One, IV 2 11
Freeman, Dora Steward — One
Freeman, David — One IV 3
Freeman, Martha Caloway — One
Freeman, Emily Hazelbaker — One
Freeman, John — One, IV 3 1
Freeman, Elizabeth M Tracy — One
Freeman, Loving A — One, IV 3 1 1
Freeman, Henry F — One IV 3 2
Freeman, I Fletcher — One IV 3 3
Freeman, Julia A Windle — One
Freeman, Ida F — One IV 3 3 1
Freeman, Leslie A — One IV 3 3 2
Freeman, Cloyd — One IV 3 3 3
Freeman, Sophia A — One IV 3 3 4
Freeman, Mary J — One IV 3 3 5

Freeman Nora L — One IV 3 3 6
Freeman William — One IV 4
Freeman Margaret Thompson — One
Freeman J Taylor — One IV 4 1
Freeman Lucinda Brown — One
Freeman George T — One IV 4 2
Freeman John J — One, IV 4 3
Freeman Martha A McCan — One
Freeman Samuel O — One IV 4 4
Freeman, Jesse L — One IV 4 5
Freeman Charles — One, IV 4 7
Freeman Mary V James — One
Freeman William F — One, IV 4 9
Freeman Edward S — One, IV 4 11
Freeman Cornelia Potter — One
Freeman Joseph — One IV 4 12
Freeman Sabina E — One IV 4 13
Freeman, J Purnell — One IV 6
Freeman, Elizabeth A Jones — One
Freeman, Andrew B — One IV 6 1
Freeman, Franklin P — One IV 6 2
Freeman, Thomas B — One, IV 6 3
Freeman Clement L V — One, IV 6 6
Freeman, Leonora Liston — One
Freeman Clarence J — One IV 6 6 1
Freeman Homer — One IV 6 6 2
Freeman Harry L — One IV 6 6 3
Freeman, Crittenden — One IV 6 7
Freeman Donie N S — One, IV 6 8
Freeman Martha J — One IV 6 9
Freeman James F — One IV 7
Freeman Sabina J Hazelbaker — One
Freeman, Minnie D — One IV 7 1
Freeman Anna J — One IV 7 2
Freeman, Mary C — One, IV 8
Freeman Joseph G — One, IV 10
Freeman Moses F — One, IV 12
Freeman, Isaac B — One, IV 13
Freeman Mary A — One IV 14
Freeman Isaac — One, V
Freeman, Jemima Moore — One
Freeman, John — One V 2
Freeman Mary J Wren — One
Freeman, James P — One V 2 1
Freeman, Thomas J — One V 2 3
Freeman Budella McCaun — One
Freeman Oran — One V 2 3 1
Freeman William — One V 7
Freeman Nancy C Munsy — One
Freeman Laura P — One V 7 1
Freeman Charles S — One V 7 2
Freeman Dottie D — One V 7 3
Freeman James F — One V 8
Freeman Mary F Walling — One
Freeman Carl V — One V 8 1
Freeman Susan — One V 8 2
Freeman Mark H — One V 8 3
Freeman, Joseph F — One V 8 4
Freeman, Nellie L — One V 8 5
Freeman James — One VI
Freeman Ann Prather — One
Freeman George M — One VI 1
Freeman Levi — One VI 2
Freeman Narcissus Smalley — One
Freeman Volney W — One VI 2 1
Freeman Anna C Ham — One
Freeman, John F — One VI 3
Freeman Belle Lilbett — One
Freeman W Shannon — One, VI 4
Freeman Rebecca A Bradley — One
Freeman Moses — One, VII
Freeman, Margaret McCormick — One
Freeman James G — One VII 2

Freeman Millie L Tracy — One
Freeman Moses J — One, VII 2 1
Freeman James N — One VII 2 2
Freeman, Harriet F Dean — One
Freeman Edwin J — One VII 2 3
Freeman, William M — One, VII 2 4
Freeman Jennie Humble — One
Freeman Joseph A — One VII 2 5
Freeman Charles — One IX
Freeman Keziah Osman — One
Freeman, John J — One IX 2
Freeman Mary M Scudder — One
Freeman Charles H — One IX 2 1
Freeman, John W — One IX 2 2
Freeman, Ettie J Hardster — One
Freeman, Ida J Shirley — One
Freeman Albert R — One IX 2 2 1
Freeman Mabel B — One IX 2 2 2
Freeman Joseph — Two
Freeman Elizabeth Higgins — Two
Freeman William — Two, III
Freeman, Tamar Beach — Two
Freeman, Joseph — Two III 1
Freeman Lias — Two III 2
Freeman Sarah A — Two III 3
Freeman Elizabeth — Two III 4
Freeman Stephen — Two III 5
Freeman Milby — Two IV
Freeman Elizabeth McCormick — Two
Freeman Nancy A — Two IV 2
Freeman William — Two IV 3
Freeman J James — Two IV 4
Freeman Sarah — Two IV 5
Fry Nancy Freeman — Two I
Fry Joseph — Two
Fry Elizabeth — Two I 1
Fry Joseph — Two I 2
Fry Louisa — Two I 3

Gumite J E Pearl Steen — One VIII 2 2 3
Gumite Charles A — One

Harris Minnie J Cox — One, IX 1 11
Harris John C — One
Harris Elsie J — One IX 1 111
Hoover Mary J Freeman — One V 3
Hoover Andrew P — One
Hoover J H P — One V 3 1
Hoover, Dora Shick — One
Hoover John L — One V 3 2
Hoover Alice L Cook — One
Hoover Jemima A — One V 3 3
Hoover Cassius L — One V 3 4
Hoover Evelyn Sayers — One
Hoover Olive A — One V 3 5
Hoover Wilbur F — One V 3 6
Hoover Flora Helvi — One
Hoover, Lulu D — One V 3 7
Hoover Emily P Freeman — One V
Hoover David — One
Hoover, Charles S — One V 5 1

Jones Dora S Wamsler — One IV 5 9
Jones John A — One
Jones Mary F Wamsler — One IV 9 4
Jones William H — One
Jones Flossie P — One IV 9 4 1
Jones Louisa Freeman — One V 4
Jones James W — One
Jones William J — One V 4 2
Jones James L J — One V 4 2 6
Jones John A — One V 4 2 7
Jones Nora Mather — One

Jones Mary E — One, V 4 2 8
Jones Margaret M — One V 4 2 9
Jones, Elizabeth H Freeman — One, VII 3
Jones, Thomas H B — One
Jones, Emma L — One, VII 3 1
Jones, James M — One, VII 3 2
Jones Martha A Liston — One
Jones Thomas C — One VII 3 4
Jones, Edwin W — One VII 3 5
Jones Alva B — One VII 3 6

Lawrence Mary E Steen — One VIII 2 2
Lawrence, Ernest L — One
Lawrence, Mildred — One VIII 2 2 1
Lawrence, Meredith Fay — One VIII 2 2 2
Layton, Ioe P Freeman — One, IV 7 3
Layton, Samuel — One
Layton, Denver F — One IV 7 3 1
Lewis Elizabeth A Freeman — One, V 6
Lewis, Levi D — One
Lewis, Nellie — One V 6 1
Lewis John F — One, V 6 2

McCall Sarah J Freeman — Two, IV 1
McCall William — Two
McCall Ann M — Two, IV 1 2
McCall William F — Two, IV 1 4
McCall, Harriet E Suttle — Two
McCall, James U — Two, IV 1 6
McCall Anna Patterson — Two
McCall, Louisa A — Two, IV 1 8
McCall Emma I — Two, IV 1 9
McCall, Louisa M — Two IV 1 9
McCormick Emma A Wamsley — One, IV 5 4
McCormick, George D — One
McCormick Edgar B — One IV 5 4 1.
McCormick, James O — One
McCormick Catherine B Freeman — One IV 7 4
McFarland Artemis Freeman — One, IV 6 4
McFarland, Isaac D — One
McFarland, Robert M — One IV 6 4 1
McGovney Maria K Cox — One, IX 1 3
McGovney, Scott H — One
McGovney Alexander H — One IX 1 3 1
McGovney, Alberthe — One IX 1 3 2
McGovney, Annie — One IX 1 3 3
McGovney William S — One, IX 1 3 4
McGovney Mary A — One IX 1 3 5
Mason, Samantha A Cox — One, IX 1 2
Mason, Christopher C — One
Mason, Sarah A — One IX 1 2 1
Mason, Elza D — One IX 1 2 2
Mason Maggie M — One IX 1 2 3
Mason James A — One IX 1 2 4
Mason, Mattie M — One, IX 1 2 5
Mason, Charles W — One IX 1 2 6
Mason, Wheeler L — One IX 1 2 7
Mason, Chester O — One IX 1 2 9
Mason, Martha M Cox — One IX 1 4
Mason, James W — One
Mason, Everett W — One IX 1 4 1
Mason, Elva M — One IX 1 4 2
Mason, Esta F — One IX 1 4 3
Mason, Arthur C — One IX 1 4 4
Mason, Katie A — One IX 1 4 5
Mason, Charles W — One IX 1 4 6
Mason, Allen C — One IX 1 4 7
Miller, Cora A Freeman — One, IV 6 10
Miller John — One
Miller Charles C — One IV 6 10 1
Miller Obada — One IV 6 10 2
Montgomery, Samuel A — One

Montgomery, Sarah M K F Freeman — One IX 4
Myers, Alice B Montgomery Stout — One IX 4 1
Myers, Franklin G — One
Neary, Elizabeth J Wamsley — One, IV 5 3
Neary, William L — One
Neary, Samuel T — One IV 5 3 1
Neary, Floyd D — One IV 5 3 2
Neary, Melvin O — One, IV 5 3 3
Neary, May F — One IV 5 3 4
Neary, Essie B — One IV 5 3 5
Neary, Lav C — One IV 5 3 6
Neary, Ann L — One IV 5 3 7
Neary, Harley P — One, IV 5 3 8

Punnell — — — Two IV 5 1

Ralston Sarah S Freeman — One IV 6 5
Ralston Wesley — One
Ralston Martha I — One IV 6 5 1
Reynolds, S Emeline Freeman — One, VII 4
Reynolds, Joseph M — One
Reynolds, Oscar F — One VII 4 1
Reynolds Jesse T — One VII 4 2
Reynolds, Maud — One VII 4 3
Reynolds, Delilah J McCall — Two IV 1 3
Reynolds, Joseph M — Two
Ryan, Sarah L McCall — Two, IV 1 7
Ryan, Christian H — Two
Ryne, Florence Wamsley — One, IV 5 5
Ryne George — One

Steen Mary Freeman — One VIII
Steen, Aaron F — One
Steen W Freeman — One VIII 1
Steen, Emma M Stipp — One
Steen, Ernest Linden — One, VIII 1 2
Steen, Clarence F — One, VIII 1 3
Steen E Watson — One VIII 2
Steen Julia E L Diboll — One
Steen, Laura Alice — One VIII 2 1
Steen, S Martin — One VIII 3
Steen, J Truman — One VIII 4
Steen Moses D A — One, VIII 5
Steen Mary Foster — One
Steen Lulu Grace — One VIII 5 1
Steen, Josiah James — One VIII 6
Steen Isaac Burl — One VIII 8
Steen, William Wirt — One VIII 9
Storer, Pauline J Freeman — One, V 2 2
Storer Fernando C — One
Storer Elizabeth B — One, V 2 2 1
Storer, Jessie P — One V 2 2 2
Stout John Cedu — One

Thompson, Susannah Freeman — One, IV 2 1
Thompson, John H — One
Thompson, Minnie I — One IV 2 1 2
Thompson, Laura B — One IV 2 1 3
Thompson, Elizabeth M — One, IV 2 1 1
Thompson Freeman — One, IV 2 1 5
Thompson Charles H — One, IV 2 1 6
Thompson, James A — One, IV 2 1 7
Thompson Rosa M — One IV 2 1 8
Thompson, Cora M — One IV 2 1 9
Thompson, Margret I Freeman — One IV 2 6
Thompson William J — One
Thompson Michael A — One IV 2 6 1.
Thompson, Ida M — One IV 2 6 2
Thompson, John D — One IV 2 6 3

Thompson, Charles C	One, IV 2 6 4
Thompson Cora A	One, IV 2 6 5
Thompson, Enza Ethel	One IV 2 6 6
Thompson Zola Jane	One, IV 2 6 7
Thompson Harley B	One IV 2 6 8
Thompson, Clair L	One, IV 2 6 9
Thompson Jesse C	One, IV 2 6 10
Thompson, Dollie O	One IV 2 6 11
Thompson William L	One IV 2 6 12
Thorp, Inez Thompson	One, IV 2 2
Thorp, George I	One
Thorp, Ray L	One, IV 2 2 1
Thorp, Harry	One IV 2 2 2
Thorp, Wilbur	One, IV 2 2 3
Tracy, Mary J Freeman	One VII 1
Tracy Joseph W	One
Tracy Elizabeth M	One VII 1 1
Tracy, Emma A	One VII 1 2
Tracy Jane F	One VII 1 3
Tracy Moses W	One VII 1 4
Walters, Austie L Blair	One V 1 2
Walters, James L	One
Wamsley, Mary J Freeman	One, IV 4 6
Wamsley, Jasper	One
Wamsley, Carey	One IV 4 6 1
Wamsley, Clara B	One IV 4 6 2
Wamsley, Elizabeth A Freeman	One IV 5
Wamsley Samuel B	One
Wamsley, William F	One IV 5 1
Wamsley Mary F McCormick	One
Wamsley, Clement L	One IV 5 1 1
Wamsley, Charles S	One IV 5 1 2
Wamsley, Damaris O	One IV 5 2
Wamsley, James F	One IV 5 6
Wamsley, George M	One IV 5 7
Wamsley, Electa Ellen	One IV 5 8
Wamsley, Allen M	One
Wamsley, Ocie Alice	One IV 5 8 1
Wamsley, Harley R	One IV 5 10
Wamsley, Nancy J Freeman	One IV 9
Wamsley, Moses	One
Wamsley, James M	One, IV 9 2
Wamsley Mary J Montgomery	One
Wamsley Pansy B	One IV 9 2 1
Wamsley, Ruth	One IV 9 2 2
Wamsley Andrew C	One, IV 9 3
Wamsley Samuel K	One IV 9 5
Wamsley Dora Montgomery	One
Wamsley Clyde O	One, IV 9 5 1
Wamsley Alton C	One IV 9 6
Wamsley, Chalmers W	One IV 9 7
Wamsley, Mary Freeman	Two II
Wamsley Isaac	Two
Wamsley, Matilda	Two II 1
Wamsley Elizabeth	Two II 2
Williams Fannie Freeman	One III
Williams, Isaac	One
Williams Nancy	One III 1
Williams Elizabeth	One III 2
Williams Jesse	One III 3
Wykoff, S Ellen Freeman	One IV 11
Wykoff George M	One
Wykoff James M	One IV 11 1
Wykoff Ann E Newman	On
Wykoff Minnie M	One IV 11 1 1
Wykoff John W	One IV 11 3
Wykoff William A	One, IV 11 4
Young Dora L Blair	One V 1 1
Young Zechariah	One
Young Theodore Ovid	One V 1 1 1
Young Ralph Elam	One V 1 1 2
Young Mary Eve	One V 1 1 3